Praise for Chris Goodrich's
Anarchy and Elegance

"[T]he most creative book on law school in recent memory."

– John Jay Osborn, Jr., *The Paper Chase*

"[A] vivid, amusing and thought-provoking description of what it feels like on the battlefield."

– Robert Heilbroner, *The Worldly Philosophers*

"[S]hould be essential, cautionary reading for budding lawyers."

– *Publishers Weekly*

"[A] masterful contribution to the literature of reportage."

– *Magill Book Reviews*

"Goodrich has scored a bull's eye."

– *The Jerusalem Post*

...and for *Roadster*

"[C]onsistently provocative and diverting"

– Chris Lehman-Haupt, *New York Times*

"Like Robert M. Pirsig in *Zen and the Art of Motorcycle Maintenance*, Goodrich uses mechanical details as springboards for thoughtful and carefully documented discussions of car culture...."

– *Los Angeles Times*

"[S]trong, crisp and clear."

– *Hartford Courant*

"[C]aptivating...reminiscent of John McPhee."

– *Publishers Weekly*

Published by Gimlet Eye Books, 80 Obtuse Hill Road, Brookfield, CT 06804, (203) 740-1789. More information at *www.faithisaverb.com*.

Goodrich, Chris.
Faith is a Verb: On the Home Front with Habitat for Humanity in the Campaign to Rebuild America (and the World) / Chris Goodrich.
p. cm.
ISBN 0-9768221-0-5
1. Spirituality
2. History, U.S.
3. Contemporary Culture

LCCN: 2005925041

IS YOUR company, organization, university, classroom, community, etc., interested in building with Habitat for Humanity? Then contact Habitat International at *www.habitat.org*. If you're interested in purchasing additional copies of *Faith is a Verb* – to use as gifts, premiums, promotions, for fundraising, etc. – contact Gimlet Eye Books at *www.faithisaverb.com*. Note: *Half the proceeds from sales of this book are given to Habitat International or local Habitat affiliates.*

Design by David Goodrich / Birdtrack Press
Cover and Gimlet Eye colophon by John Goodrich

Faith is a Verb

On the Home Front
with Habitat for Humanity in the
Campaign to Rebuild America
(and the World)

Chris Goodrich

Here's to
'Infectious Habitat!'
C Goodrich

GIMLET EYE BOOKS

Also by Chris Goodrich
<www.chrisgoodrich.com>

Anarchy & Elegance:
Confessions of a Journalist at Yale Law School

Roadster:
How (and Especially Why) a
Mechanical Novice Built a Sports Car
From a Kit

Front cover photos: Habitat house in snow, Danbury, Conn. Credit: Chris Goodrich.
Truss-raising, Jacksonville, Fla. Credit: Kim MacDonald / Habitat for Humanity Int'l.

Back cover photo: Habitat volunteers, Durban, South. Africa. Credit: Gregg Pachkowski / HfHI.

This book is dedicated to
Habitat homeowners, volunteers, and contributors
all over the world.

Contents

How vain it is to sit down to write
when you have not stood up to live.
– Henry David Thoreau

[To] have faith in something is an
inducement not to dormancy
but to action. To me, *faith*
is not just a noun but also a verb.
– Jimmy Carter

Overture

We are swarming. There's no other way to put it: we are swarming like worker bees, or worker ants, beyond thought, driven by enthusiasm. Bud's cutting two-by-tens to length, for joists; Corey's slapping down particle-board decking, creating the subfloor; Gordon's securing the deck with a nail gun, Margo's installing metal bridging between joists, John's building headers for the stairwell, Pablito's handing out nails like candy, Rich is unloading lumber, Pieter's hammering in joist hangers – and that's only half today's crew. We're a little village, and appear to be racing against time, but in fact we're just happy to be working. Between building codes and lack of money, a tax fight with the city of Danbury and a change in construction management, zoning regulations and false starts, it's taken a year to get this far... but now, at long last, we're building again.

Margo's a first-timer on site, and far luckier than she knows. Putting in the deck at 16 Patch Street – it's a quintessential Habitat experience, when the work is steady, the need for volunteers high, and progress quick and conspicuous. At this rate, *you think,* we can build an entire neighborhood! A town! Finish off dilapidated, dangerous housing in Connecticut, in the world, in no time: move on to hunger, to poverty itself! *Deep down we know better, of course, but the optimism, the satisfaction, is palpable... even if it is the product of effort-born endorphins, of construction sweat, of working outside on a gorgeous fall day. How often, without doubt and without hesitation, do you find yourself wearing a white hat? Doing something not just because you want to, but because it is, without question, the right thing?*

I've been volunteering with Habitat for five years now, have worked on sixty-odd houses, so I should be stepping back. Hang up my hammer, become a full-time go-fer and supervisor and cheerleader, let new people like Margo do the hands-on work; make sure they never experience a dull moment, constantly accomplish, always return. How else will the twice-a-years become every-monthers, the every-monthers every-weekers? How else will we get the job done, build a hundred million houses? We've only begun, really, only scratched the surface; we need more bodies, more sweat, more commitments....

I should kick myself upstairs, in short, but I can't. Who knew that building walls, laying block, nailing shingles, could be so much fun? That working for nothing, helping someone else, could be so rewarding? (Below, Housatonic Habitat volunteers install the house deck in Danbury, Connecticut.) That acting altruistically could be... no, forget that idea, it's misleading to imply selflessness. Quite the opposite: this is, perhaps, the most selfish thing I've ever done, for what I do at this Habitat site actually matters. *When I reported for magazines, wrote for a major newspaper, I felt so significant, a shaper of issues and maker of tastes...but those jobs seem hollow to me now, insubstantial. This is real work, significant work: here I feel in the thick of life's marathon, a "player." I'm no longer amusing people to death (to use Neil Postman's summation of our entertainment-driven culture); with a million other people, and more, I'm applying the Habitat brake, I'm trying to turn this ship around.*

I love the smell of sawdust in the morning, the recoil of a pneumatic gun, the snap of a taut chalk line. Sinking a nail with three blows, sharpening a pencil with an open blade, reaching for a tape measure and having it fall to hand. I feel, today, a relapse into 'infectious Habititis,'

a disease that compels victims to spend every spare moment on Habitat worksites, participating very personally in the building of an American dream. Because those long-forgotten, long-repressed, childhood-superhero fantasies are true: we can save the world. The only catch being that we have to do it ourselves, with our individual sweat and blood.

Introduction

Thomas Jefferson, who had rejoiced with every other American patriot when Cornwallis surrendered at Yorktown in 1781, believed the American Revolution had been betrayed within a decade. The Federalists had begun to consolidate power in the nation's capital; Alexander Hamilton, Washington's Secretary of the Treasury and Jefferson's chief rival, had pushed through a national bank favoring industrial and corporate interests. Jefferson genuinely believed that "the tree of liberty must be refreshed from time to time with the blood of patriots & tyrants" – so he wrote in 1787, on the eve of the French Revolution – but wasn't ready to call for a second rebellion, not yet. Disillusioned by the compromises and crassness of politics, the backroom deal-making and up-front malice, he retreated to his beloved Monticello, where "I have my house to build, my fields to farm, and to watch for the happiness of those who labor for mine."

Monticello, of course, bears little resemblance to the homes built and sold by Habitat for Humanity International. It's huge, for one thing: a mansion, far beyond the means of the average American of any era. But like Jefferson himself, whose political instincts were deeply, radically democratic, Monticello represents a deeply held American dream – that hard work and dedication can bring great visions to fruition, against whatever odds and opposition. Monticello, moreover, doesn't call attention to its architect, doesn't say I'm-so-stylish with every face and shadow; it exalts not the individual but the culture, the political system, which allows such individuals to think, daydream, experiment. Jefferson often used the term "the spirit of 1776," and that's what Monticello embodied – America writ small, a celebration of the freedom to choose, to let talent find its natural limits.

Like most Virginia planters, and despite the all-men-are-created-equal rhetoric of the Declaration of Independence, Jefferson was a slave-owner. But he recognized the contradiction...one reason he designed neo-Palladian cottages at Monticello for favorite slave families. The cottages (drawing by Jefferson, right) were never built, a casualty of Jefferson's public years and his deep personal debts, but they capture his vision of a conscientious, community-based America, a nation intended as a model for the world. Jefferson rarely left Monticello after retiring from the presidency in 1809.

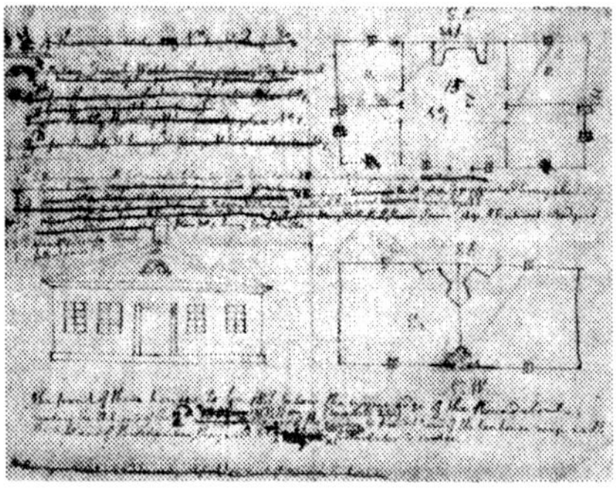

Historian and biographer Joseph Ellis mocks the suggestion that Monticello was the third president's "own personal City on a Hill," but to a significant degree it was just that – an attempt to create at his own home the kind of society he couldn't inspire, through appeals to reason and fair dealing, his fellow countrymen to build. Jefferson had tried to expand the rights of mulattoes in Virginia in the early 1770's, had harshly condemned the slave trade in his original draft of the Declaration, but with limited success. Jefferson "hated" the compromises inherent in politics – he used that very word – so it's easy to see Monticello as an always-under-construction, do-it-yourself, lead-by-example democracy standing in stark contrast to both an ever-growing, power-oriented, help-your-friends federal government and a newly released, sky's-the-limit, wheeling-and-dealing business culture.

The philosophy that drove Jefferson to create and withdraw to Monticello, in other words, isn't so different from the philosophy that drives Habitat today. No, volunteers don't mutter "We want to recapture the values of our Founding Fathers" at every opportunity: they simply show up by the tens of thousands, day in and day out, because they believe wealth is meant to be shared, not hoarded or wasted or conspicuously consumed. "Life, Liberty and the pursuit of Happiness" didn't represent to Jefferson the chance to get rich quick, to sit on the porch drinking and gambling, as many of his Tidewater relatives did; it was the chance to build from scratch the finest, fairest country the world had ever known.

Jefferson dreamed of an agrarian America, one populated by yeoman farmers and small-scale craftsmen. That's why he made the Louisiana Purchase despite his opposition to federal power, why he hoped to give every landless American family a fifty-acre homestead. And while Jefferson won the image battle with Hamilton – Monticello and the Declaration live on, his bitter antagonist is remembered for dying in a duel – he lost the ideological war. Had Jefferson devised a time machine and transported himself to the 21st-century (a big "if," considering his major invention was a more-efficient plough), he would recognize Habitat volunteers and homeowners as latter-day yeoman on a new philosophical frontier. Politicians may develop blueprints, but they don't build nations: people do, with personal commitment and belief, with bare and calloused hands.

Today's Habitat "home-makers" aren't blazing trails in the wilderness. In truth, they aren't even building: they're *re*-building a nation, a world, one house and family at a time. It's homesteading on asphalt on an unparalleled scale...and is serving to reclaim, almost incidentally, an American faith that's been dormant for decades. The Habitat philosophy, by putting practice before theory, rejects the sharp edges of both capitalism and socialism, taking the best of each and adding large doses of Christianity and "good ol' American know-how." And it seems to work: to date Habitat volunteers have built more than 50,000 houses in the U.S. and 125,000 more around the world, creating safe, affordable shelter for nearly a million people.

That's a drop in the bucket on a planet of 6.5 billion, 1 billion of whom live in poverty. As Jefferson and others have noted, the Americans who fought in the Revolution were likewise outnumbered, but won their freedom through unshakable, unstoppable faith. Habitat volunteers aren't at war, but they are fighting for a better America – by drawing sketches rather than swords, striking nails rather than people. And they're finding, too, that they're becoming better individuals themselves, because hanging wallboard with one-time strangers, tying rebar with unfamiliar neighbors, produces a far more satisfying Saturday than shopping at

the mall. As Jimmy Carter, Jefferson's successor and regular Habitat volunteer, once put it, "Working with Habitat is never a sacrifice. It's become one of the greatest blessings of my life." Jefferson, the master of Monticello, would envy Carter (shown above, with wife Rosalynn, at the 2000 Jimmy Carter Work Project in New York City) his post-presidential career…especially if he could design some Habitat housing himself.

One

Responsible Madmen

Millard Fuller is in Texas, but he could be anywhere in the world. Another city, another state, another steam-table lunch – or is it catered? Fuller, the founder of Habitat for Humanity, doesn't notice, and doesn't care, and not only because he's skinny as a board. He's on a mission: to get people to give a damn.

"I hear you're going to build 50 houses in Dallas this year," he tells the audience, a mix of local politicians and business executives, Junior Leaguers and nothing-better-to-do retirees. The usual suspects for a boring civic luncheon...except for the teenagers and middle-school children, and the sweaty types with torn blue jeans and t-shirts and work boots, and the skin tones ranging from pasty white to dark chocolate. And, of course, the prison inmates. The convicts have been working with Dallas Habitat for a few years now, having discovered that helping people can be more fun than hurting them, that you can get as much by giving as by taking. The prison-outreach initiative is one of many started by Habitat – I've installed inmate-built porch railings with the Bridgeport, Connecticut, affiliate – and there's no end in sight. Before the decade's out expect to see Habitat houses built by Left-Handed Zoologists and Knock-Kneed Sports Announcers.

"Why not 52?" Fuller continues in his go-ahead-underestimate-me Alabama drawl. "You don't want to build 50 houses and leave the other two weeks of the year out. That's just unheard of!" The audience guffaws, knowing they're on the hook, and that Fuller, beneath the

humor, isn't kidding. The Dallas affiliate has completed more than 200 homes in less than 15 years, but that's not enough for Fuller. Of course, 2,000 wouldn't be enough, either, nor 20,000 – not since Fuller found himself saying, on a San Francisco radio station in 1981, that Habitat's goal was "to eliminate poverty housing from the face of the earth." The station's switchboard lit up...and Fuller knew he was right to Think Big.

"The United States, the richest country in the world, has millions of people living in poverty housing," says Fuller (shown above in Nevada in 2004), a fact he's shared thousands of times, with hundreds of thousands of people. "This is not an impossible problem, this is a solvable problem. We have the money, we have the know-how: all that's lacking is the will to do something about it." He points to Japan, Norway, Sweden: those countries have very little dangerous, unsanitary, substandard housing, so why should America? Fuller – who looks more like a Mayberry, R.F.D., grease monkey than chairman of a $700 million organization – is preaching to the converted; he was introduced by Dallas' mayor, Ron Kirk, as "my kind of saint."

A man in the audience – wearing a coat and tie, a banker, perhaps, or a real-estate developer – asks a pointed question, suggesting Fuller may be running a "giveaway" program. "Habitat isn't a charity," Fuller shoots back. "We don't have clients, we have partners. People who want a Habitat house must pitch in and paint and hammer and work alongside our volunteers. We call it 'sweat equity.' They buy these houses, they pay a mortgage like anyone would – but a mortgage they can afford, because Habitat doesn't charge interest, doesn't make a profit. We call it the 'Bible finance plan.' It says in the Bible that if you loan money to a poor man, you shouldn't charge him interest."

Fuller finishes, and receives his usual ovation – not standing, this time, he's tired and a little off his game. He greets a few old friends, shakes a lot of hands, and minutes later is off again – to

Butte or Las Vegas or Pittsburgh or New York, Bolivia or Ethiopia or Vietnam or Bulgaria or Guatemala (where the girl at left lives, in a Habitat house), wherever he's been called to celebrate an affiliate anniversary, a 100th house, a fund-raising goal, a week-long 'blitz' build. "I have a house," he likes to say, "but I live in airports" (sounding a bit like Jefferson, who complained that political duty forced him to abandon "everything I love, in exchange for everything I hate"). It's profoundly odd that the head of the world's largest non-government home-builder is rarely home himself, but to Fuller, home is a frame of mind: one Habitat t-shirt reads "Oh, we have a home, we just need a house to put it in." Fuller will be home, *completely* home, when all those imagined homes become real.

Housatonic Habitat, based in Danbury, Connecticut, is perpetrating a fraud. That's what it feels like, at least, because no one on God's green earth would believe this is a rehab. A couple days from now the house (shown below before the tear-down) will consist, in its entirety, of two eight-foot, see-through side walls bearing bits of broken clapboard; it will look like an "after" picture from Tornado Alley. A rehab? Hardly; but the city doesn't really care, for the powers that be are glad to see a wreck coming down. Instead of waiting, fruitlessly, for an absentee landlord to pony up for services rendered – city water, more than $20,000 worth, had been flowing inside nonstop for years, due to a burst pipe – in twelve months the mayor will be able to shake hands with a new, resident taxpayer.

This project, a duplex on 16 Patch Street, is Housatonic Habitat's eighth home in Danbury, tenth in the area. And Fuller's reassurances notwithstanding – "The first house," he tells newborn affiliates, "is always the hardest" – the process isn't getting easier, because Fairfield County (think Westport, Greenwich, Darien, New Canaan) is one of the most expensive places for housing on the entire planet. Land costs a bundle, is regulated within an inch of its life, and the neighbors are often, well, spoiled. The city took six months to waive the outstanding non-payment-of-services lien; the zoning board cut no slack, permitting a duplex only if the existing footprint was maintained; the construction committee, limited to one structure, had to custom-design the homes rather than employ an off-the-shelf plan.

Ten "affordable" houses...and we haven't built the same one twice! Henry Ford would rap our knuckles and say "Give 'em anything they want, so long as it's 900 square feet on a slab with two closets and a 7/12 roof."

And now Pablito's holding his head, having been beaned by a falling rafter. (He's at right, sanding a wall at a later date.) Pablito's okay, just has to sit awhile and rub . . . but we won't tell his wife Linda (or OSHA) about the incident. Linda's also a volunteer, and I'm not sure she should learn what really goes on at a Habitat site. Some things you shouldn't know. . . .

We're in "demo" mode this month – demolition – and as usual, behind schedule. The roof will come off today, maybe a wall or two, depending on how reckless, and wreck-ful, we feel. Pablito's already back at work...and I'm no longer making fun of our retired dentist (song of the day: "Don't Worry, Be Gordon"), who's wearing a beat-up bicycle helmet for protection. In fact, I'm going back to the car to retrieve a hard hat, and to get thicker gloves, because the shingles are full of nails. Not as many as the new house will have, of course, being built by cautious amateurs. *When a Habitat house burns down*, long-time volunteers joke, *you can sell the ruins as scrap metal.*

Jim M., a volunteer-turned-part-time-paid-crew-leader, has suggested leaving the front part of the roof alone, because the affiliate is, in fact, cheating. We still don't have a demo permit, so we pretend we're "remodeling"...but the act wouldn't fool a five-year-old, because the roof looks like the Jolly Green Giant sat on it, repeatedly. I'm reminded, coming back from the parking area, what a structural engineer said decades earlier about my own first home, in Berkeley, California. *There are two ways to build a roof,* he said a few days before I signed the purchase contract. *This is neither one of them.*

From the street I could see the west wall bowed out at least a foot off vertical, and the east wall – what was left of it – even farther from vertical, seeming to hang on for dear life. I was on the stairs, wondering when the slanting steps would fall into the basement, when Bill cut through a rafter...and half the roof, with a great *cra-a-a-a-ck* and *whoosh,* smashed to the floor. I checked myself for stray nail holes...and grinned, because I love doing demo. How often do you get to break things on purpose, smack something around for the common good?

It's nearly noon, and no major injuries – a victory in and of itself, for we're a bunch of out-of-shape, middle-aged-and-older, one-step-from-Florida amateurs, and not as skilled as we like to think. Yes, Phil's worked construction professionally – but hey, maybe he's just acting, at the drop of a nail apron he breaks into Brando's "coulda been a contenda" speech (the whole thing, not just a few lines). Bud A.? He's an excellent rough carpenter, and I figured he was a retired journeyman until someone referred to him as "The *Rev.* Bud A." (Don't call him Horton, his given name, or you risk eternal damnation.) Pablito's a retired mechanical engineer, and I'm always asking his advice...but he doesn't talk much, most days, perhaps self-conscious about his Filipino accent. I idolize the guy – he's incredibly patient, and thoughtful, and everyone's guardian angel – so I'm convinced he noticed problems with the roof and decided to take one for the team. Yes, home construction is a young man's game...but for zero dollars an hour, you don't hope for strapping beefcakes in their rent-and-beer-money prime. You get old guys like us – Housatonic Habitat's Thursday Crew, Danbury's answer to the Dirty Dozen.

I've worked on many homes with these guys, in various combinations and permutations, and they've become my bridge club, my Fraternal League of Amateur Builders (ignore the acronym, please). I've gone on week-long Habitat builds with some, to fund-raisers with most, and begun to appreciate why Millard Fuller says Habitat is "more than houses." A family in need gets a non-leaky roof, sure...but that's the tip of the iceberg. We're building something bigger: a new community, a new perspective, maybe even a new ethic. Who knew that working for nothing could be so satisfying? That "market value" and "intrinsic worth" operate in entirely different spheres, are barely on speaking terms? That "going off the grid," economically speaking, opens up bigger, entirely new worlds? My crew-mates walk their talk...and in this media-saturated, money-rules, talk-is-cheap age, that's no small thing.

Sorry, I'm drifting. I've been reading about Monticello recently (photo, below right), and wondering about its lovely, round-windowed dome (*How did Jefferson hoist it, how could he afford it?).* Right now, though, I need to focus: the collapsed section of roof – eight feet by ten feet, we bit off more than we could chew – has to be sliced-and-diced, because its weight is pushing out the side walls, and we can't shore up the remaining roof until the fallen section's out of the way. So suddenly, like responsible madmen, we're stripping shingles, roofing slats, tin flashing, rafters suffering

from dry-rot and wet-rot, tar paper that tears like, well, paper. It's cartoonishly comical: five minutes earlier we were in first gear, but now we're in fifth, our leisurely demolition transformed into a flurry of activity. We fling the shingles and wood into wheelbarrows, dump the detritus into the parking area (if only the dumpster were a few feet closer!), and deploy a come-along ratchet and poly rope to winch the walls into something approaching vertical.

Not a bad morning's work, but not a job well done, either. Today we've been embarrassingly sloppy: didn't use the proper equipment, cut too-large roof sections, failed to add safety braces, didn't insist on hard hats and safety goggles, took far too many short cuts. We'd done all kinds of silly, stupid things...but what sticks in my head is the phrase *The perfect is the enemy of the good.* If we waited until we were ready, we'd never be ready; waited until somebody else gave the okay, we'd never get started; waited until the demolition permit arrived, we'd cool our heels for a week, a month, a year. Rules, sometimes, are for sissies.

Our half-deaf crew chief – Jim N., who spent far too much time under the sagging roof feigning inability to hear cries of 'Jim, get out of there, please!' – has fetched lunch from the local deli. The sandwiches are tasty, not because they're good but because we feel good. And I'm thinking there's no place I'd rather be, even though – maybe because – I'm exercising none of my hard-won professional skills, am putting my college education to no use whatsoever.

Jane Smiley, in the novel *Good Faith*, captures nicely the deterioration of the American Dream. Not so long ago, the dream was to have a place of one's own: to buy a home, fix it up, settle down, start a family, and enjoy the fruits of one's labor. Sure, a house was also a long-term investment, but it was a sign of stability above all, of going beyond hand-to-mouth existence. And at one time, that was enough: if you had the basics, and a few spare dollars, you were no longer poor…and that meant you were rich, in ease and satisfaction if not in net worth.

Smiley picks up the house-as-dream story in the 1980's, when the idealism of the 1960's has evaporated and Ronald Reagan's morning-in-America sunniness rules the national culture. Joe Stratford is a real-estate agent in Pennsylvania, a few hours from New York City, and quite happy selling nice homes to nice people. But former IRS agent Marcus Burns moves to town, and soon Stratford is caught up in a plan to develop much bigger houses at much bigger prices in a full-service, self-contained, Rich-B-Us community. Burns' idea is "can't miss," or so the locals soon believe, and while Burns isn't as charming as Henry Hill in "The Music Man," that hardly matters: he's playing to greed, not vanity.

The dream he's selling, moreover, seems to have substance – concrete and glass, wood and asphalt, green lawns and white picket fences. In fact, of course, Burns is playing a shell game, because people don't actually need expensive, 10,000-square-foot homes (a

"McMansion" at right, from the website www.swineotopia.com), however much they might want hotel-lobby living rooms, however many times they've taken celebrity-crib tours via television. Burns' proposed development collapses before a single house is built, its would-be Trump flees with the investors' money…and Stratford, like countless one-time straight-shooters, realizes he flew too close to the sun.

Burns is not a lovable rogue – but he's difficult to dislike, too, because he didn't intend to steal, he simply got caught up in a fast-and-loose era in which smart people, and even not-so-smart people, were *supposed* to get rich. What makes the story appalling is Burns' fundamental assumption – that houses are *not* homes but high-profit merchandise, to be sold at prices far beyond their intrinsic worth, to people who can't afford them, with amenities buyers neither need nor understand and didn't want until they were told they *should* want them. Although real-estate transactions are based on the "good faith" of the novel's title, Burns' faith is limited to markets, and the conviction they always go up. He's a speculator, in short…and to get rich he doesn't actually need to own property, because he can depend on other people's avarice, their belief in upward mobility. He exploits the desire for wealth, already primed by images of moneyed ballplayers and entertainers, and demonstrates – so it seems – how a middle-class Joe can become a millionaire with very little effort.

That wasn't the America Jefferson had in mind when he wrote about "Life, Liberty, and the pursuit of Happiness." The more common phrase at the time was "life, liberty, and property" – Sam Adams cited that triad in a 1772 tract, and George Mason did the same two years

later, while also referring to "pursuing and obtaining happiness and safety" – so it's clear Jefferson wanted to articulate a value system that transcended physical possessions. But you wouldn't know it from most history books, which misinterpret not only Jefferson but John Locke as well (portrait at left), the philosopher who formulated the life-liberty-property ideal. Critic Norman Podhoretz has even claimed that Jefferson used the phrase "the pursuit of property" in his first draft of the Declaration – a re-writing of history that suits modern sensibilities, but has no basis in fact.

Jefferson had no aversion to property: in fact, he was one of our most "acquisitive" presidents, if you believe biographer Fawn Brodie. What he objected to was idle property – property for property's sake, used to produce power and status rather than food or necessities. That's what his maternal relatives did, and for whom – with a few exceptions – he had little use. Jane Jefferson was a Randolph, a clan known for plantations and politics, for producing "the Adam and Eve of Virginia" and dabbling in the slave trade, which goes some way toward explaining why Jefferson barely mentions his mother in his voluminous writings.

His father, by contrast, he portrays in heroic, Paul Bunyan-like terms...though fails to mention that Peter Jefferson was once outwitted, and perhaps humiliated, by a Randolph. The future president's father was a self-made explorer and surveyor (that's his map of the Virginia territory, right), and hoped to homestead 1000 acres on the Rivanna River with his new bride Jane, but one William Randolph – a good friend of Peter's, cousin to Jane, and heir to 57,000 Virginia acres – beat him to the punch, filing a claim for 2400 acres two days before Peter submitted his paperwork. William sold 400 of those acres to Peter at a large discount – so the story goes – after learning of his friend's disappointment.

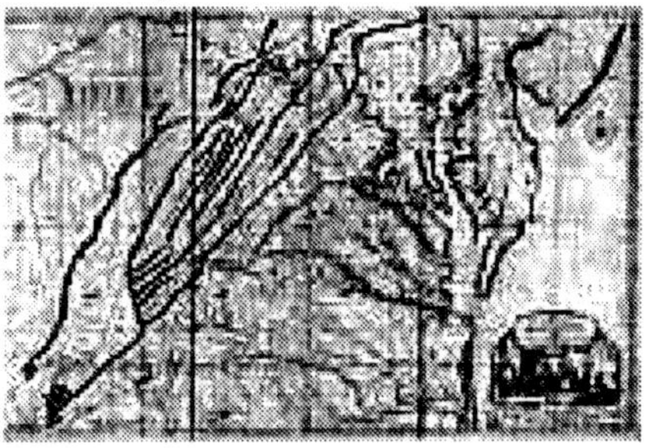

Was William Randolph's pre-emptive claim part of an elaborate joke? Did Thomas Jefferson suspect his mother of complicity? Was the land competition a coincidence, unexpected? The historical record remains silent...but the experience surely gave Peter Jefferson an up-close-and-personal look at the advantages of inherited wealth, ready cash, and a business-first approach to life. If son Thomas knew the story, he had good reason to build a don't-tread-on-me home on land that nearly slipped through his father's fingers, and to be suspicious of those with much property who sought still more. Jefferson remained wary of large land-owners throughout his life, noting, while Washington's envoy to pre-revolutionary France, that much real estate outside Paris was owned by nobles and only used for hunting. How was it possible, he asked James Madison in a 1785 letter, for so much land to sit idle, unproductive, when it could create employment for others? That "so many should be permitted to beg who are willing to work, in a country where there is a very considerable proportion of uncultivated lands?" In such a nation, he wrote, "it is clear that the laws of property have been so far extended as to violate natural right."

That view sounds radical today, even in Habitat circles, but was not unusual in its time. And Locke, though practically deified in right-to-property circles, would have agreed with Jefferson, for his "life, liberty, property" formulation is rife with caveats. While individuals retain property rights in their own bodies, Locke argued, the non-human world – Nature – is God's property, and only when someone "added value" (in the modern jargon) to something could he claim to "own" it, because then he had "mixed his labour with it, and joined to it something that is his own, and thereby makes it his property." And even this qualifier had a qualifier, for Locke further argued that "no man but he can have a right to what that is once joined to, at least where there is enough, and *as good left in common for others*" [Italics added].

Jefferson believed in "the fundamental right to labor the earth," to improve one's existence through the sweat of one's brow. So does Norman Podhoretz, of course, and every other defender of property rights. The difference? Locke's second qualifier – his belief that man could curb his greed, could share natural abundance. But that seemed a forlorn hope in America, though Jefferson hoped otherwise: the American push for "more," as exemplified in Marcus Burns and adopted, incrementally, by Joe Stratford, ensured that wealth became a sign of virtue, even intelligence. And thus the stage was set for what biologist Garrett Hardin called "the tragedy of the commons," in which common resources, once used in moderation by all, are used up, or monopolized, by the conspicuously consuming few. By Mark Twain's Gilded Age the idea of leaving "enough, and as good left in common for others," was a negative attribute, for the "manifest destiny" of the U.S. was to control and consume, expand and own. Once you sat down at the table, you were expected to leave nothing behind, not even a crumb.

Habitat addresses that imbalance by making private property more public, by stressing "enough" rather than "excess." Perhaps the pendulum is swinging back to the middle, as people recognize that the thrill ride of too-muchness destroys humanitarian instincts, natural rhythms, wherever it takes root. "That's one problem with big houses," says Fuller, who's walked through scores of mansions while raising funds. "Sometimes you can't find the bathroom – or when you do, you don't recognize it."

Two

Fresh from the Stream

Millard Fuller was not impressed when he first met Clarence Jordan. He was, in fact, disappointed: Jordan looked "ordinary" in a plaid shirt tucked into faded overalls, and Fuller, being six-foot-four, was indifferent to Jordan's six-two. Jordan might be a scholar and social activist, a philosopher and visionary, but to a man from Alabama's capital city, Montgomery, he seemed a run-of-the-mill cotton farmer.

But Fuller knew he should disregard appearances. He had arrived at Koinonia Farm, a few miles outside Americus, Georgia, in spiritual crisis, forced to recognize only a week earlier that his life was a sham, a crock. And his fall – so it seemed to outside observers – was precipitous: the previous year, 1964, Fuller had been told by the treasurer of Fuller and Dees Marketing Group that he was officially a millionaire. For a moment Fuller celebrated... then sent the treasurer back to work, saying they'd better start hustling toward his next goal, reaching ten million dollars. Fuller and Dees was already the largest cookbook publisher in the U.S., already selling millions of products every year – toothbrushes, tractor cushions, candy, anything on which you could put a logo – but that wasn't enough. Fuller didn't just want *more*, he wanted *everything*.

He was living, in short, the American Dream. With one minor problem: he was married to his work, not his wife, and Linda Fuller had had enough. One Saturday evening in November 1965, Fuller arrived home late (from the office, of course) to hear Linda say she was leaving. The announcement wasn't a complete surprise – Fuller had taken note when Linda murmured a year earlier that she no longer loved him – but he was shocked nonetheless. The chauffeur and maid, the his-and-her Lincolns, the summer place on the lake, the mansion on twenty acres we're building – sheesh, what else is there? To all appearances the Fullers had everything they could want, that anyone could want; they were the envy of Montgomery.

"I'm going away for a while," said Linda, Fuller's steady since she was 17. "I don't know if we've got a future together." Being six-foot herself, she had been attracted to Millard's height, and his get-up-and-go, but that energy wasn't directed at her anymore. She'd recently taken a college course on ethics, and the big Lincoln didn't seem quite so shiny, her enormous walk-in closet so important. Linda (shown at right, at Koinonia, in 1971) flew to New York City the next day, to talk things over with a minister far from hometown gossip.

For a week Fuller juggled work and parenthood. He left the office at five; he put the couple's two children to bed for the first time in years. And he was haunted by one particular memory – that he and Linda had once promised to "outlove" one another. It was something he couldn't avoid thinking about, because the Fullers had put the vow to paper a week before their wedding, she writing one word and he the next. The covenant hung above every bed they'd owned together, including the king-size in which Fuller now slept alone.

He called New York again and again, and Linda – knowing the power of Fuller's salesmanship – wouldn't come to the phone for days. When she relented, Fuller begged to see her, and she couldn't say 'No.' Fuller flew to New York on a company-chartered airplane, and although Linda did not welcome him with open arms, she saw the fear and pain in his eyes ("it was like death walked in the door," she has said). They talked, they walked, they went to a movie at Radio City Music Hall – "Never Too Late," as it happened. Afterward they wandered on Manhattan's busy midtown streets, ending up on the steps of Saint Patrick's Cathedral.

And there, on Fifth Avenue, Linda prepared to end her marriage. She would confess to a long-term affair, prompting Fuller to walk away forever. How could he do otherwise, since only business relationships seemed to matter to him? Since he cared mostly about money and status and *things*, not home and hearth and family? (Even on this trip, though Linda didn't know it at the time, Fuller had put business first: before landing at LaGuardia he'd flown to upstate New York to meet with a toothbrush supplier.) Cash was king in Fuller's view, wives anything but profit centers: either Fuller had been too self-centered to notice Linda's desperation and distance, or simply didn't care.

But Fuller didn't walk away, for in that week of solitude he'd begun to question his most basic assumptions. Was this truly the life he wanted, always grasping for the next lead, the next deal? Did he really want to be an absentee father, an absentee husband, an absentee home-owner? He also confronted a growing personal anguish, one he'd long repressed. *Why am I so full of anxiety, can't seem to breathe right, like my lungs are failing? Why do I feel myself a stranger in church now, as if I don't belong? Could my cousin be right – that 'bidness' has changed me for the worse?* "I realized," Fuller would later write, "that I had indeed become a virtual stranger in my own home"; that the trappings of his 'good life' were just that – ornaments, form without substance, eye-catchers serving mostly to hide the owner's hollowness.

Fuller, to Linda's surprise, embraced her. Moments later, while other tourists admired the Thanksgiving decorations going up on Fifth Avenue, they huddled in a storefront weeping.

That night the Fullers talked – and sang, and prayed – until dawn. And when the sun rose, a radical idea had taken shape in Fuller's head. He'd sell his businesses, his law practice; he'd spend his time in service rather than self-promotion, making his *family* happy rather than his accountants.

It was a drastic plan, and one with which Linda wholeheartedly agreed. Fuller wouldn't just cut back; he'd abandon business entirely, liquidate his assets and distribute the proceeds to the people he'd heard about in church long ago – the hurting, the forgotten, the people who needed money in ways he hadn't for years. He resolved, in short, to start anew, understanding for the first time the destructive force of avarice, of equating material possessions with personal success. "We had gone too far down the wrong road to be able to correct our direction with a slight detour," Fuller wrote in *Love in the Mortar Joints*, which he wrote soon after founding Habitat. "We simply had to go back and start all over again, but this time we would let God choose the road for us."

The road, within days, led the Fullers to Koinonia Farm and Clarence Jordan. (The name's pronounced 'Jerdon,' as Americans learned when Clarence's nephew Hamilton became Jimmy Carter's chief of staff.) The Fullers had retreated to Florida immediately after their reunion, intending to repair their relationship and contemplate the future, but on their way home Fuller remembered that friends had recently settled in a Christian community not far from their Montgomery route. The detour made sense, since the Fullers, soon to be ex-millionaires, weren't sure how to go about serving God; perhaps the community's founder, said to be a great man and a deep thinker, could provide direction? The Fullers had no idea, then, that Jordan would change their lives to the very core, nor that they were encountering a latter-day Martin Luther. Jordan is a little-known figure today, but his writing says very plainly – as we'll see – that many modern churches follow money more than Jesus, put capitalist ethics before Christian.

The Fullers, arriving in Koinonia's rustic dining hall, found Jordan sitting on a wooden fruit crate deep in conversation with two other lunch guests – a retired chaplain and a newspaper reporter from Columbus, Georgia. When the subject turned to the materialism of American culture, the love of cash and flash, Fuller was mesmerized. Jordan (shown at right) seemed to understand his situation as no one had before, as Fuller himself did but vaguely; he put Fuller's yearnings, and regrets, in context. When the reporter said wealthy people in Columbus seemed to lack "a sense of stewardship," of responsibility to their community, Jordan replied, "They are money addicts. They're just like folks who have been hitting the bottle. They have already had more than it takes to make them drunk but they just can't quit." Those people, Jordan said, were "money-ics," unable to help themselves and always looking for their next 'hit.'

Fuller was all ears, Jordan having sketched exactly his recently disavowed self. And as the conversation continued, Fuller couldn't get enough, because Jordan – who had seen the Fullers drive up in one of their Lincolns – also seemed to understand the Bible, and God, and the nature of goodness, better than any person, any preacher, he'd ever heard. Fuller hoped to learn more about "moneyism" right then, but early December was Koinonia's busiest time, as the farm survived by selling Christmas candy by post. Fuller was sure he could help, having made millions in direct mail, but was disconcerted

to learn that Koinonia's candy trade was the result of happenstance, not planning. Koinonia was founded on pacifism, race integration, and a loose socialism, so through much of the 1950's the farm was harassed with death threats, incendiary bombs, shotgun and machine-gun fire. (A 1937 Klan rally in Atlanta is pictured above.) Making lemons out of lemonade, Koinonia – a working farm community to this day, and still selling nuts and candy – sold its pecans by mail, using a slogan coined by Jordan: "Help us ship the nuts out of Georgia!"

If the Fullers spent the night, Jordan said, they'd find time to talk. So they did stay – that night, and the following thirty as well, in what Linda once described as "a little un-insulated house that was about the size of one of our bathrooms back home." Jordan's talk of "faith in action," Fuller realized, was exactly what he was looking for…even if it did mean sleeping next to Ku Klux Klan bullet holes.

For a month Fuller and Jordan packed candy and milked cows together, all the while talking about the nature of success and the meaning of faithfulness, about the Crucifixion and the Klan. Within weeks the Fullers were no longer millionaires, Fuller having commenced his financial divestiture. None of the money went to Koinonia: on that Jordan insisted, because he refused to accept gifts carrying even the shadow of a string. He quoted the New Testament often and by heart – sometimes in his own translation, for he considered most renditions stiff and lifeless, inaccessible to ill-educated sharecroppers. "Put no value on earthly things," says Jordan's Jesus in the Sermon on the Mount, "which worms and rust consume, and which thieves break into and steal.... For your values and your character are wrapped up together." That made sense to Fuller – and so did Jordan's Jesus when he said, in Matthew's gospel, "[A] pig can go through a knothole easier than a rich man get into the God Movement."

Life at Koinonia, to Fuller, was revolutionary. People at the farm not only studied Jesus and his teachings, they aspired to *live* like him. And that, of course, was the point. Like Jesus, they were setting an example; were living as if talk, even Christian talk, was cheap.

Church-goers around the world knew many Bible stories by heart, Jordan told Fuller, but turned stone deaf when asked about the stories' relevance, their meaning. Sure, said Jordan, "We'll talk about loving enemies in the Sunday school class, but on Monday we've got to make bayonets, grenades, missiles.... We'll love them after they're safely dead." Yes, "That's a nice story about Jesus turning over the tables of the money changers in the temple in Jerusalem, but don't turn over any of the tables of *our* money changers in *our* temple!" For millions of Christians, Jordan argued, going to church was purely for show, not so different from going to the country club, the symphony, the dentist. You went because other people went, because your parents did, because you always had.

Fuller the Money-ic, for years, had buried his doubts about Southern Christianity. Here, though, was someone willing to take a stand – not unlike Rosa Parks a decade earlier, who had galvanized the civil-rights movement by refusing to sit in the back of a Montgomery bus. Fuller was uncomfortably familiar with that story, for when a bus full of Freedom Riders (like the one just below) arrived in Montgomery in 1961 to continue Parks' protest, he watched a white mob beat up every black it could find. Dees and Fuller, the sister law firm of Fuller and Dees Marketing Group, agreed to represent one of the vigilantes, and its fees were paid by the Klan and the equally segregationist White Citizens' Council.

Such dubious compromises are in Fuller's past…and that of his former partner, too. Morris Dees, two years after buying Fuller's share of their partnerships, became a civil-rights activist himself, founding the Southern Poverty Law Center and targeting, above all, the Klan.

Fuller was exhilarated by Jordan's vision, and convinced God had led him to Jordan's knee. But for what purpose? To what end, and with what tools? Jordan had ideas and suggestions, but none sparked Fuller to say, "Aha, that's my life's work!" He wasn't a farmer-theologian but an entrepreneur, a salesman, a deal-maker; what could he do for Koinonia? To further Jordan's heaven-on-earth reverie, to make his "God Movement" a reality? Fuller's talents were many – his marketing prowess would soon transform a lackluster Koinonia pecan cookbook into a hot seller – but temperamentally, he was Jordan's antithesis. Jordan was cast in the small-is-beautiful, think-globally-act-locally mold, while Fuller had the businessman's conviction that bigger is better, that the local could be "grown," in modern business-speak, into the global. Koinonia suited Jordan to a T, reflected his innermost beliefs: surely there was another Christian-infused project that suited Fuller equally well?

The answer would come, but took years to materialize.

It's impossible to overestimate Jordan's influence on Fuller and Habitat for Humanity. Fuller recognized as much in 1999, calling Jordan, on the thirtieth anniversary of his death, Habitat's "spiritual father" and re-naming a Habitat building the Clarence Jordan Center. Jordan reminded Fuller, as noted above, "your values and your character are wrapped up together": that you are what you believe, and beliefs aren't worth much if they go unpracticed.

It's likewise difficult to imagine Koinonia, or Habitat, being launched anywhere but the American South. Jordan's faith-in-action philosophy brought home the contradictions between two of the South's most hallowed traditions – rock-ribbed Christianity and die-hard racial prejudice. If you truly believed Jesus' teachings, you couldn't be bigoted; if you were truly bigoted, you couldn't be Christian. The road forked, and like the Fullers in New York City, you had to choose one path or the other.

Fuller and Jordan (together at Koinonia, below) both grew up in small, Deep South towns – Jordan in Talbotton, Georgia, and Fuller in Lanett, Arkansas, 70 miles to the west and just across the Chattahoochee River – where many whites prospered and most blacks did not. But only Jordan, it seemed, felt something was wrong with Southern society, sensed his culture's internal dissonance. He knew from

an early age that what he heard in church on Sunday didn't jibe with the world outside – and he wasn't one to avoid an argument.

"Clarence would fight with anyone in the family," his brother Frank told Jordan's biographer Dallas Lee, a former journalist and Koinonia resident. Clarence's combativeness earned him the nickname "Grump"...and, so the family thought, a place in law school. In fact it was Clarence's brothers Frank and Robert who became lawyers, Frank practicing in Talbotton and Robert going into politics – his reward, thought Clarence, for abandoning Christian principles. When Clarence asked Robert to help Koinonia after it was firebombed, he refused, saying (Clarence remembered) "Why, if I represented you, I might lose my job, my house, everything I've got." Like Fuller with the Klan in the 1960's, Robert took the path of least resistance...and went on to become a deacon in his church, a state senator, and chief justice of the Georgia Supreme Court.

For a time Clarence did consider law, because even as a child his sense of justice was close to the surface. When his father, a bank and general-store owner, verbally abused a black delivery boy for coming to the front of the house, ten-year-old Clarence berated his father to his face. And since the Jordans lived near the center of Talbotton, only a hundred yards from the county jail, Clarence learned about Southern justice on a daily basis. Walking home from school, he'd see convicts in ankle bracelets, and befriended many while eating the cornbread and fatback offered by the jailhouse cook. The vast majority of the chain-gangers were black, and Clarence noticed early on that white prisoners rarely suffered the worst punishments – beaten with whips, locked for hours in a makeshift pillory, tied to a rack-like device called "the stretcher."

Jordan soon understood that the major "crime" of many convicts was being poor and black. The idea was driven home one night in 1924, when Jordan, then twelve, heard groans issuing from the lockup. (Years later he would delight in noting that the jail was designed by one John Birch, grandfather of the missionary for whom the fervid anti-communist group – Jordan called it the "John Besmirch Society" – was named.) Jordan identified the groaner as a convict named Ed Russell, and the man tightening the stretcher's block-and-tackle as the chain-gang warden – the same man who'd gotten carried away singing bass during "Love Lifted Me" at the previous evening's revival meeting.

At that moment, Jordan said in adulthood, such hypocrisy made him "bitter against God." He dreamed, writes Lee, "of going off to the state law school and then raging back into the county like a savior to see that justice was done in the county jails and work camps." But Jordan's avenging-angel fantasy was indeed a fantasy, because race issues, in the 1920's and 1930's, simply weren't addressed. Millions of Southern youngsters sang in Sunday school

Jesus loves the little children,
All the children of the world.
Red and yellow, black and white,
All are precious in His sight,
Jesus loves the little children of the world

...but few besides Jordan recognized the clash of values, and even fewer took it to heart.

Jordan, after graduating from high school in 1929, enrolled in the University of Georgia's agricultural program. His views toward racism hadn't changed – he still wanted to do battle – but Jordan had concluded that his relatively privileged life, while providing good intellectual training, was hindering his real-life education. He simply couldn't understand black culture, black needs, black issues, by reading books: he had to see black life, experience it, for himself. He didn't dye his skin, as John Howard Griffin did, decades later, to write *Black Like Me* (cover of recent

hardback edition, at right), but took up a typical Southern black occupation – farming. His father, J.W. Jordan, didn't like the idea – *Why go to school for that?* he asked. *I'll buy you a mule, and you can start right now!* – but eventually relented. He paid Clarence's undergraduate bills for nearly four years, until J.W.'s Bank of Talbotton collapsed during the Great Depression.

Jordan, at college, participated in every extracurricular activity imaginable – fraternities, debating teams, drama clubs, band, YMCA events, numerous honorary societies, the student newspaper, the Baptist student union, the Reserve Officers Training Corps. Although relentless social involvement is unremarkable in the South – Baptist church programs can occupy students from dawn until bedtime – it's difficult to read about Jordan's college years without picturing a square peg alongside a round hole, fruitlessly attempting to slip in.

Fuller would lead a similarly busy existence at the Southern universities he attended, but without exhibiting a shred of doubt. He was unwavering, even then, in his pursuit of wealth; he and Dees ran a dozen businesses in college and law school, perhaps the most profitable of which involved real estate. One summer Fuller worked construction in Flint, Michigan, laying blocks, pouring foundations, doing carpentry, and generally improving his building skills. He bought a beat-up Ford, drove it home, and after graduating from Auburn University and enrolling at the University of Alabama School of Law, formed a partnership with a fellow law student – Morris Dees – to rehab dilapidated apartment buildings near campus.

They generated working capital, Fuller writes, by trying "any crazy idea that looked potentially rewarding" – selling mistletoe, holly wreaths, doormats, and most importantly, student directories. Yes – Fuller and Dees were crazy like foxes. With personal student information already in hand, the partners wrote every parent and offered to deliver a 'Bama cake on their children's birthdays…and cleared, Fuller reports with glee even today, two dollars a cake.

If Fuller saw opportunities in any given system, Jordan saw injustices. He tried to fit in throughout college, but after his father's bank went under, confronted a hole to which he couldn't conform.

He applied to Kentucky's Southern Baptist Theological Seminary (the original Norton Hall, since torn down, is shown in postcard below), in Louisville, and not because he'd lost interest in farming. He'd simply concluded that race problems ran deeper than agriculture, deeper than economics. With an "ag" degree he could show sharecroppers how to increase productivity, overcome inefficiencies, rotate crops, improve market timing…but to what end? So they could adopt a dog-eat-dog ethos, spend more time and money drinking in bars? Buy the same china and sheets and nice cars, the televisions and kitchen gadgets, as the middle-class folk? Money and possessions, as Jordan had seen from his own family's experience, didn't produce happiness, satisfaction; it produced, if anything, the desire for more, and more, and *more*. "There had to be something extra somewhere," Jordan said of his change in direction. "I was driven in a desperate search for spiritual resources."

With money tight, Jordan spent the summer at ROTC boot camp. He'd joined the corps' cavalry unit in college, and since he excelled at horsemanship – as at most things – arrived at the seminary with a second lieutenant's commission. Once more, though, Jordan's personal views clashed with a culture he hoped to find a good fit. In his free time he studied the Bible, and certain ideas – particularly those from the Sermon on the Mount – stayed with him. During cavalry training one day, as he slew dummies with saber and pistol, he imagined himself as the straw enemy while his ears echoed with Jesus' *But I say unto you, love your enemies, bless them that curse you.* Jordan realized, right then, that he was trying to serve two masters, and resigned his commission within the hour.

Southern Baptist Theological Seminary, often called the "granddaddy" of American religious-education institutions, is Bible-centered and generally conservative. So Jordan, inevitably, found no peace there, either. The president of the seminary referred to Robert E.

Lee as "the greatest Christian since Paul," and although admitted to breaking bread with a black deacon in Brazil, pointedly refused to do the same "in Birmingham." Jordan, by contrast, did just that, which both troubled and relieved fellow seminarians and teachers. *If Clarence wants to do the dirty work, well, why not let him?* By 1939, Jordan's last year in graduate school, he was directing a small mission project in a largely black section of Louisville, the West End. The mission was housed in what had been a famous bordello: the staircase banister bore a devil's head carved in wood, and Sunday school was held in rooms where hookers entertained johns.

Here Jordan absorbed first-hand the hardships of urban poverty. He found the mission's original name, the "Sunshine Center," condescending and Old South, so changed it to the Fellowship Center: started an outreach program that attracted parishioners with movies, choirs, local black preachers; organized meetings among clergy regardless of skin color. Jordan went to extraordinary lengths to bridge the racial divide, knowing his parishioners had little reason to trust whites, even white preachers. So when a black girl was raped by a white man, and a neighbor with an iron pipe threatened revenge, Jordan stepped forward, put his head on a table, and said, "If a white man must die for this rape, let it be me. Do it now."

Jordan spent so much time with one black congregation that he applied for membership. That didn't bother his fellow worshipers, but horrified his own church's higher-ups. Jordan noted in his journal, sarcastically, the birth of a new church doctrine – the need to expurgate from the New Testament "all those pages which proclaim the universality of the Christian brotherhood."

But Jordan found supporters in Louisville, too. Some professors expected seminarians to think for themselves, to grapple with the Bible on their own. Jordan was encouraged to explore the friction between Southern religious theory and Southern religious practice – how the Old Testament could be cited as supporting racism and segregation, how the New Testament's focus on mercy and justice could be spun into meaninglessness. Most significantly, Jordan mastered ancient Greek, enabling him, as he later put it, to retrieve Jesus' teachings "fresh from the stream." From there it was a small step to grasping that many preachers, from America to Africa, Britain to Bali, were selling their congregations a bill of goods.

By the time he graduated from Southern Baptist, with a doctorate in Greek New Testament, Jordan was well outside the Southern Baptist tradition. And he knew it; as early as 1936 he told his fiancée, Florence (shown with Jordan at right), "If you want to be the wife of a pastor of the First Baptist Church, you don't want to marry me." The organized church could never accept his personal theology because the organized church was, in Jordan's view, a large part of the problem. Many churches and church officials served themselves as much as God, spending money on steeples and vestments, travel and embellishments, rather than parishioners (and other people) in need. As Jordan would later say, on hearing of a church leader who occupied "the swankiest suite in the swankiest hotel" for a conference, "I'm not too sure that child is in the image of the Almighty God whose boy was so poor he had nowhere to lay his head."

Jordan had studied the New Testament in its original language, the vernacular, "street" Greek known as *koine.* (Fuller says he never saw Jordan read from an English-language Bible, only from the Greek.) And what he found in the *koine* version was a Jesus markedly different from the one he'd heard about in the church of his youth, for this Jesus' views were radical. (Jordan knew, of course, the word "radical" originally meant "fundamental"; like "radish," it's derived from the Latin word for "root.") Standard translations of the New Testament, Jordan realized, were produced and distributed by church or church-approved hierarchies, which altered and interpreted Jesus' teachings as well as spread them. Jesus was often portrayed as a man of The Word, but Jordan understood Jesus as a man of Action for whom words were only means to an end. Words were problematic: they could be treacherous and misleading, empty substitutes for work, change, improvement. Jesus, and Jordan, preferred the Deed – and what deed was more telling, more effective, than allowing oneself to be crucified for a fabricated crime?

Jordan didn't believe, of course, that martyrdom was required of Jesus' followers. But he did think Christians, through action, should embody Jesus' words, just as Jesus incarnated (a key word in Jordan's lexicon) the word of God. "How can you go and say to people," Jordan argued in one anti-segregation sermon, "'That which is not a reality among us, we declare unto you' – a brotherhood which we cannot practice...?" Christians who talked the talk, but didn't walk the walk, were Christians in name only, because they acted as if faith required only lip service.

Brotherhood – that was Jordan's focus, because the lack of it seemed a spreading cancer. In Louisville he and Florence had formed, with a handful of summer missionary students, a *koinonia* – a word meaning "community" or "fellowship" (and also derived from the word *koine*). The spirit of Jesus, in Acts 2:44-45, through Peter forms a *koinonia* in which he and his disciples "had all things in common: and sold their possession and goods, and parted them to all men, as every man had need." (At right, a logo of Amherst Koinonia Church in Massachusetts.) In Jordan's Kentucky version – and at Koinonia, as originally organized – members did likewise: they pooled their incomes, ate meals together, and decided jointly on the outlay of common funds. The phrase "From each according to his ability, to each according to his needs" may have been set to paper by Karl Marx (by his translator, in truth), but the idea is fundamentally Christian.

Jordan's first *koinonia*, being composed mainly of students, disbanded after a few months. But in 1941, in the early years of World War II, Jordan read a Baptist newsletter article in which the author, Martin England, argued that *koinoniai* might, indeed, prove man's salvation. England, a Baptist minister on furlough from Burma, had found his mission work handicapped by the racism of white Christians from the U.S. "If the barriers that divide man, and cause wars, race conflict, economic competition, class struggles, labor disputes, are ever to be broken down," wrote England,

> they must be broken down in small groups of people living side by side, who plan consciously and deliberately to find a way wherein they can all contribute to the Kingdom according to their respective abilities. Suppose there were some Christian employees and employers, whites and Negroes, farmers and merchants, illiterate and school teachers, who were willing to enter into fellowship to make a test of the power of the spirit of God in eliminating the natural and artificial barriers that exist now....

England, clearly, was thinking along the same lines as Jordan, and each felt God's hand at work on discovering they both lived in Kentucky. The men met, talked, and – inevitably – acted. Within months they formed Koinonia Farms, Inc., what Jordan called "our own little alternative to war."

The farm's goal, as the two preachers noted in a fund-raising brochure, was explicitly spiritual and evangelical. But it was inescapably political as well, to their everlasting dismay: compromise and back-scratching, deceit and violence, were not part of the early-Christian ethos. The farm would provide an "apprenticeship in developing community life" for aspiring followers of Jesus, and would also teach local blacks, laymen and clergy, about ways to "conserve the soil, which we believe to be God's holy earth" (Locke's view, once again). Koinonia Farm would be a grand, godly experiment, an inter-racial, peaceable commune dedicated to helping those "desperately searching for a way in the wilderness" – to anyone who believed, with Jordan, that the United States wasn't living up to its spiritual, largely Christian ideals.

The search for "typical" Southern farmland (Koinonia peanuts, on the right) led the partner-preachers to Alabama, then back to Georgia. They found appropriate property an hour south of Jordan's birthplace – 440 acres in Sumter County, Georgia, halfway between Americus and Plains (towns of major importance to the Habitat story). Buying the property (a modern peanut patch at Koinonia is shown on the next page) proved, in the end, relatively easy: a well-off, sympathetic businessman gave Jordan and England the down payment. Possession was

complicated, however, because the tenant family who lived in the farmhouse didn't move on, as expected, at the close of the harvest season. The man (white, as it happened) was curt and proprietary, but the preachers, having staked their souls on community and neighborliness, could hardly turn the family out. For weeks Jordan and England shared a single room in their newly purchased house, and were vastly relieved when the family departed in November.

The locals, at first, regarded their new neighbors with amusement. The preachers, for one thing, had little capital; and although Jordan held an agricultural degree, and England had worked on farms as a child, their learning was mostly academic. In Koinonia's early days,

Jordan said, he climbed on the farmhouse roof every morning to learn what the day brought. If the neighbors were plowing, the preachers plowed; if they were planting, the preachers planted. Had the locals known of Jordan's rooftop research, they would have laughed heartily...and certainly did on seeing the newcomers prepare their vegetable garden. One preacher guided the plow, while the other, strapped into traces, pulled. (In photo above, mules pull people, not ploughs, at Koinonia.)

Before long, though, Koinonia became a source of resentment. A Negro frequented the place – a normal, unthreatening sight until the locals learned that the man, once a sharecropper, was a paid employee. The gossip and innuendo started, to the effect that Jordan and England – "outside agitators," as they would eventually be called – needed watching.

The talk turned to anger when neighbors realized the black man not only worked alongside his white employers, but *ate* with them, too – at the whites' insistence! When challenged, Jordan said he was doing only as Jesus asked: treating all men as brothers. But his words fell on deaf ears, and the confrontation came soon after. One day in

1943 a car full of men drove to Koinonia and asked for Jordan. The leader announced his membership in the Ku Klux Klan, adding – to his regret – "we don't allow the sun to set on anybody who eats with niggers."

The phrase played to one of Jordan's intellectual strengths – serious thought disguised in levity, the truth of his words not registering for minutes, days, months. Jordan told Dallas Lee that he grinned his best grin, grabbed the man's hand in his own bear paw, and replied, "I'm a Baptist preacher and I just graduated from the Southern Baptist Seminary. I've heard about people who had power over the sun, but I never hoped to meet one!" Koinonia won a reprieve, and the day's victory was sealed when the head Klansman acknowledged that his father, too, was a Baptist preacher.

Much worse would come in the months and years ahead, with more locals every day convinced that Koinonia was a serious threat to the Southern way of life. The civil-rights movement lay far in the future, but the very word "equality" sent shivers through the dominant culture. Hundreds of thousands of whites depended on blacks for their middle-class lifestyle, as a local school official acknowledged when Koinonia representatives volunteered to create a school-bus system for black children. "Niggers do our work for us around here," he replied, "and if we educated them they will all move away, so I don't intend seeing them educated." If the racial equality encouraged by Clarence Jordan caught on, traditional Southern society (a minor part of it illustrated at right, with a Klan songbook) would indeed be dead, never to rise again.

Three

"The Only Game in Town"

In *Flatland*, a fable published in the 1880's by Edwin Abbott, a native of Flatland describes his journey into Spaceland. It's an eye-opening visit, because the narrator, a mathematician named A. Square, couldn't conceive of a culture being different from his own. He's lived in only two dimensions, as a geometric figure on a flat plane; has known nothing but surface, has no concept of thickness, of depth. Despite his blinders – laughably obvious to modern readers – Square considers himself an enlightened polygon. (Below, the original cover of the book.)

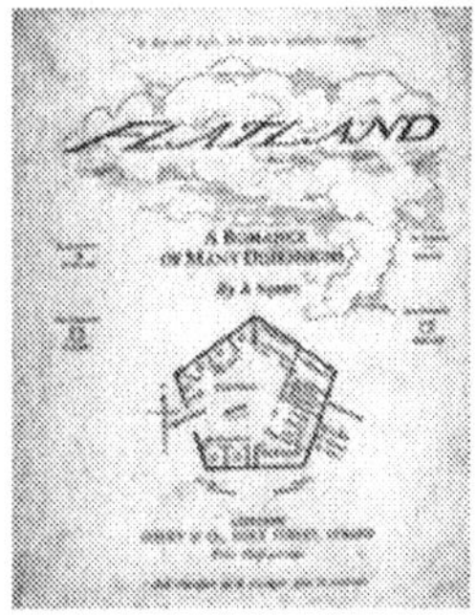

He learns better, though, when visited by a figure from Spaceland. The stranger calls himself a Sphere, though Square, limited by his two-dimensional mind-set, initially believes him to be a Circle… and no amount of reasoning can dissuade him. Sphere notes that appearance can change – a coin lying flat on a table appears circular when seen from above, he says, but seems a line when viewed from the side – but makes no headway, for Square, like most Flatlanders, considers talk of "three dimensions" to be heretical. Sphere, frustrated, lifts Square into the third dimension – "up" – where he admits to seeing "a Line that was no Line; Space that was not Space." Terrified, Square shouts

'Either this is madness or it is Hell'...but is soon convinced the third dimension does, in fact, exist. Returning home, he can't keep his discovery to himself – and writes Flatland in prison, sentenced to a life of incarceration for speaking seditious, immoral thoughts.

Abbott, a minister as well as a mathematician, composed the tale for both religious and didactic purposes. (Left, Sphere being perceived as a circle.) It illustrates effectively that you can't "see" what you haven't been trained to see, that the unknown is beyond

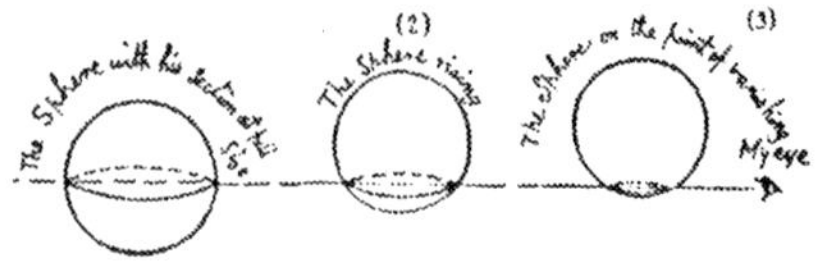

language, beyond preconceived ideas. Does a lack of experience, of mindpower and imagination, mean a fourth dimension (or a ninth, or a twenty-third) cannot exist? No. Abbott, at bottom, is proposing the existence of God – that the inability to see a higher power, a higher dimension, proves nothing besides the limitations of human consciousness. *We learn what we want to learn, and deny what doesn't fit; we see what we want to see, and ignore the rest.*

I had no idea, when I first volunteered with Habitat, that it would become my Spaceland. It hardly seemed capable of drawing me into another dimension: what could be more straightforward, obvious, than hammering nails in wood? Than building simple homes, which man has done for millennia? (Right, an illustration of perspective.) I hoped to encounter intriguing complications

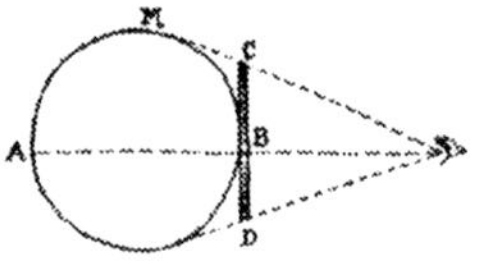

– bureaucracies and regulations, craftsmanship and learning curves – but they wouldn't compare to my previous lives: studying law and learning to write, building a car from a kit and making sense of modern literature. I was an old dog, a known quantity: I could grow, but I wasn't going to change my point of view.

Boy, was I wrong.

My first Habitat house was in Newtown, Connecticut. It was nothing like the Habitat sites you see on television, in magazines, where brigades of multi-colored volunteers swarm over a cramped, urban jobsite for a thirty-home 'blitz build.' No: a few months earlier the lot had been an untamed, emerald meadow, complete with grazing horses. In my youthful, 'green' phase in California, two decades past, I might have protested development of such an idyll...but now, as a parent and wage-earner, I understood the trade-offs, the compromises, of adulthood.

A chestnut stallion -- Newtown is known for its farms and riding trails – wandered in a neighboring pasture, but the Habitat property was a construction zone. The lot was littered with felled trees and piles of dirt, heavy equipment and fat-tired pick-up trucks. For all that, though, you could imagine, once the homes were finished, the return of bucolic life.

Which also meant you could forgive passers-by for thinking "'*Habitat*'? Sheesh, that house is gonna be nicer'n mine!!!" Housatonic Habitat hadn't intended to build such a pleasing home, but local zoning regulations, and the lack of buildable lots in the Danbury area, forced its hand. Hundreds of volunteers were getting impatient – to swing hammers, yes, but also with the affiliate, because Housatonic had completed only one home since its founding seven years earlier. Faced with "over-building" its homes or not building at all, the affiliate chose the former...and if that meant putting up relatively spacious, farmhouse-like homes in the Newtown style, well, so be it. The board of directors understood the irony – the less Habitat homes looked like Habitat homes, the more Newtown liked it – but hoped to outlive the contradiction.

The first Philo Curtis Road house (below, seen from the second house), did look vintage 1920's – tall and narrow, with a front porch for summer evenings and many windows for the changing seasons. The design had numerous constraints – Habitat policy doesn't allow garages or picture windows, and its floorspace maximum (1200 square feet for a four-person family) was Newtown's minimum – but the house looked neither pedestrian nor cheap. It fit the neighborhood...though in a rather different way than Peter Eckert, Habitat's architect, first envisioned the home. He'd hoped to transform an existing, concrete grain silo into a new kind of affordable housing, but the Habitat board turned him down flat.

"It was definitely doable," says Eckert, wistfully. "Maybe another time."

Roger Authers, a business-development associate of IBM who ran the affiliate's publicity committee, said I might be disappointed by my first visit to a Habitat jobsite. He certainly was: Roger was sent home minutes after arriving at Housatonic Habitat's very first build site, due to the non-delivery of construction material. (It wasn't the last time he wondered when the affiliate would get its act together.) I was luckier, for I found the Newtown site not only active but the labor agreeable. One crew had corralled wheelbarrows and was poised for yard work; a second crew was installing rafters – two men on ladders receiving lumber handed up by a third, who had cut the rafters to length on a table saw. I watched as he maneuvered a circular saw to notch the rafters at one end, creating a "bird's mouth" that captured the top of the side wall.

The process wasn't as straightforward as it appeared. As a rule, professional builders cut the rafters for a roof all at once, since they employ experienced carpenters, own the proper tools, and have done the same roof before. A Habitat roofer, by contrast, is an amateur, building quite literally on the work of other amateurs; the walls aren't exact, the ridge beam imperfectly set, and the tools, very likely, are dull, dirty, beat up, and poorly used. Each of the Newtown rafters, as a result, was a custom job, varying in length up to an inch or more, with many of the bird's-mouths ragged and the plumb-cut, at the rafter end, far from plumb. The variation wasn't dangerous, and you wouldn't notice it on the completed house, but I was already thinking that Habitat homes, like laws and sausages, were something you shouldn't see made.

I inserted myself into the process at the least-skilled level – gofer, between the heavy-set rafter-cutter (I never learned his name) and Roger, who was on the installation crew. I'd arrived late, around 9:30, so the "best" jobs were taken; but that was fortunate, for I considered myself to be an intern studying a medical procedure before attempting it myself (only later did I learn most of the other volunteers were interns, too). Soon, however, I was up on a ladder on the second floor, toe-nailing rafters into the ridge beam where someone had made 24-inches-on-center pencil marks. Within the hour I manned the power saws – not because I was a terrible rafter-hanger, but because the cutter thought I should give it a go. "Learn by doing," he said. "It's the best way."

He marked the lumber with a carpenter's pencil, and I cut the ends off with the chop saw, making sure to slash right through the line. That degree of accuracy wasn't essential, but I wanted to impress the guy...and in due time grasped that he was both keeping an eye on my work and training me in crew-leader "best practices." He wasn't just building a roof: he was building a team. If I showed minimal competency, and willingness to listen, he'd welcome my return; and if I had fun, was given responsibility and allowed to do different things, I would return. That was part of Habitat's appeal – the fact that volunteers, being totally dependent on each other, had to treat one another well, learned to play their cards to mutual advantage. A volunteer could walk away at any time, for any reason: no one could be bought off, sell out, for money had no value on site. Skilled or unskilled, experienced or inexperienced, we regarded ourselves as equals, and dedicated to the same goal.

The rafters on one side of the roof were in by the coffee break (courtesy of the local Dunkin' Donuts). I was both thrilled and shocked – thrilled at being able to contribute despite my ignorance, and shocked at...well, being able to contribute despite my ignorance.

Larry Coleman, the site supervisor, used the break to talk to the group about Habitat. He didn't begin with a prayer, fortunately – one reason I was late, unwilling to hold hands with strangers in a demonstration of unity before a god I didn't believe in. Larry (photo, left, showing his Habitat colors) simply described Habitat's work, and the pleasure he took in working with the future homeowners, the Jeffreys. He introduced Sarah Jeffreys, who grinned – and I suddenly placed her as a waitress at a local restaurant. I might soon be building, I realized, for the bagger at the grocery store, the clerk at the donut shop, the nursing assistants who helped deliver my children – any of the hundreds, thousands of families who could barely afford to live in one of the most expensive housing markets in the U.S. We think of the "disadvantaged" as an amorphous group, as

"those people" we help through civic organizations or at Christmas, but they're not a "group" at all: they're neighbors and acquaintances. I could be building, months from now, a home for my babysitter, my driveway-plower, my son's teacher.

When people ask Fuller about the cost of starting a local affiliate, Habitat's founder replies, "You got a dollar?" Because that's all you need, he says – plus some deeply committed people, unquenchable faith, and endless patience. It's an effective pitch, soft-pedaling the massive effort that a newborn affiliate requires...and he's right about the money. Habitat, with its unique vision, reliable blueprint, and cheerleading-squad enthusiasm, regards money as almost beside the point, nothing more than a tool; its "business plan" assumes capital is all but compelled to follow the organization's win-win, breakthrough concept. And at bottom Habitat is a business, an investment in the community, in the nation, in humanity. The returns may not be immediate, or even economic, but they do come.

Fuller's entrepreneurial approach permeates every affiliate. I sensed it from the first few Housatonic Habitat meetings I attended: that the sky was the limit, the organization was changing the world, that we were lucky to be in on the ground floor. *This is what it must be like*, I thought, *at dot.coms in the Roaring '90's – the confidence, the we're-all-in-this-together attitude, the unquestioned belief in progress, in future success. Obstacles will arise, sure... but we'll solve 'em, come what may.*

The start-up comparison held more truth than I first imagined. Housatonic Habitat was, in fact, nearing a crisis point, one brought on by inexperience in the building trades and the difficulties inherent to home-construction in wealthy areas. It's a common Habitat syndrome: a once-optimistic affiliate screeching to a halt, unable to reach critical mass, to find a rhythm and flourish.

Hopes were high when the affiliate was chartered in 1991. Danbury had a few notorious drug dens, a few 'bad' streets, and was thrilled to learn that Habitat was "going local." The city had already condemned a number of properties for safety violations or non-payment of taxes, and eventually provided the brand-new affiliate with a run-down house on drug-plagued Elm Street – a demo job, the chance to start from scratch.

The acquisition and approval process was painfully slow. Professional builders were willing to help out, but most had paying jobs, and day-to-day management was left to wet-behind-the-ears part-timers. Yet optimism seemed justified; money wasn't so hard to come by, nor volunteers, once the local Habitat's founders tapped into their churches and employers. Hundreds of people were willing to help, for they envisioned not only a physical monument to their public-spiritedness, but actually *building* that monument, that house, with their own hands, their own sweat and blood. The combination makes Habitat virtually unique, and remains key to its appeal. As one local rabbi said, when asked why he built homes with a Christian organization, "Well, it's the only game in town!"

When push came to shove, though, construction proved problematic. From the beginning Habitat headquarters supplied a number of standard house plans, but few suited New England; most Habitat projects are in the South and other warm regions, and could be built – since you didn't need to worry much about insulation – on concrete slabs. Moreover, many qualified volunteers wanted to help with the design – architects, contractors, the occasional carpenter – and each had his or her own reasons for getting involved in the project, not all of which were selfless, or aligned with simple, decent housing. The affiliate's founders were savvy enough to say 'Of course, we'd love your help!' when skilled volunteers showed up...but had no idea how difficult it would be to mesh professionals with amateurs, non-profit regulars with for-profit, get-with-the-land-rush builders, Habitat true believers with gee-this-sounds-like-fun one-timers.

Five years passed before Housatonic Habitat completed 112 Elm Street. The four-bedroom house has flaws – the windows were too small for its broad face, as you'll note in the photograph on the right – but in 1996 Juan Gonzalez moved in with his wife and three children, leaving behind a small apartment where cockroaches sometimes crawled over the baby at night. The Gonzalezes, despite the delays, have been goodwill ambassadors for the affiliate ever since, paying their mortgage on time and turning the house into a

model home. "I promised myself that when Habitat turned over the key I would do my best," Gonzalez told the local newspaper before the family's fifth Thanksgiving dinner at their Elm Street home (turkey, plus dishes from his native Mexico). "I didn't want Habitat to think they chose the wrong person." The neighborhood remains marginal – the yard is edged with a chain-link fence, to keep out bottles and needles and riff-raff – but a beachhead was made, a dream fulfilled.

The affiliate, by contrast, didn't do so well. Most of its founders were gone before the house was completed, frustrated with the slow pace, the diffuse management, the lack of follow-through, the amateur mistakes and constant "re-dos." And the affiliate was so focused on building homes – or at least *trying* to build homes – that it neglected to build a future for itself. New blood arrived, and new donors...but most slipped away, disillusioned or annoyed and even angry, often wondering *Who's in charge here, anyway?* And in truth, no one was in charge – not the founders, not the president, not the board of directors – because of the nature of the organization. Every Habitat affiliate is a community effort, succeeds only when hundreds of individuals add their pieces to the jigsaw puzzle...and without homes to build, tasks to perform, those puzzle pieces went unused, unplaced, did not become part of a larger social pattern.

So when Newtown offered a three-acre lot to Housatonic Habitat, the affiliate's prayers were answered . . . or so it seemed. The final outcome, years later, was happy, but getting there almost killed the affiliate, its board failing to notice that this gift horse had very bad teeth.

Housatonic Habitat's low point came during a board meeting in August 1998. The first Newtown project already seemed like the House from Hell when Larry, the site supervisor, brought more bad news. A volunteer surveyor had worked from out-of-date documents: the access street, Philo Curtis Road, was actually three feet higher than indicated on the site plan. Since the house was situated well below the street, on the side of a gentle hollow, Larry needed thousands of yards of fill to meet state regulations for driveway slope.

Larry, a former TWA pilot who managed commercial construction projects during the work-week and Habitat's Newtown development on Saturdays, estimated that it would cost $15,000 – including truck, driver, and dirt – to get the fill on-site. Habitat would probably get the fill free, because Newtown was anxious to reduce a huge mound of excavation soil deposited on city land, but Larry was less optimistic about its delivery. The town would likely charge for that – in part because the affiliate's scatter-shot approach to construction had raised hackles as well as eyebrows. Larry had been trying to line up a contractor to dig the foundation for the site's second house...and if Habitat rescheduled the guy one more time, Larry said, "he'll probably take out his .45 and shoot me."

Larry was kidding, mostly. But he knew another delay was inevitable, because he'd discovered, while staking out the second lot, that the site plan itself was skewed. "The guy told me he'd amend it," Larry said, "but I suspect this isn't revised: I can't smell the ammonia." He sniffed at the blueprint, continued. "That's where we are, or I should say, where we aren't. I can't tell from this" – he slapped the plan – "where to put the second house."

The news was a bitter pill because the board still hoped the first house would be finished by Thanksgiving, the latest in a string of projected completion dates. The project had gone wrong from the get-go, despite strong backing from Newtown's first selectman, Herb Rosenthal, who had seen gentrification increase the price of housing so much that few homes could be classified as affordable. (Nearby towns, as the photo at right indicates, were even less hospitable to affordable housing.) Habitat appreciated Rosenthal's support, but the lot had been donated to Newtown with the understanding, by some parties, that it would be preserved as open space. With a large town park just down the street, and the town close to triggering Connecticut's controversial affordable-housing statute, Newtown gave Habitat the nod.

The housing statute, intended to prevent over-concentration of the poor in urban areas, allows developers to side-step local zoning ordinances if a town fails to make at least 10 percent of its housing "affordable." But the law – modeled on similar legislation in New Jersey, Massachusetts, and California – has often been abused, for it allowed developers to say, in essence, "If your town doesn't approve our low-density, luxury townhouses, we'll invoke the affordable-housing law, put in high-density, low-income housing…and think of all those kids moving in, they'll blow out your school system! Is that what you want?" And developers aren't the only ones to play hardball: cities have responded by saying, "Fine. On second thought, what this town really needs is open space, so we'll take your property through eminent domain. Here's a check for its fair-market value, unless you want to meet again in court." The result? No housing at all, less land to build on, higher real-estate prices, and racial and economic prejudice camouflaged under a 'green' banner.

Many Philo Curtis residents, when the news of the Habitat project got out, were livid. They objected to their street being chosen for "affordable" housing, assuming that low-cost housing would lower property values. (In fact, that's rare with Habitat homes, since the organization's presence signifies a neighborhood on the upswing, and because Habitat homeowners have an emotional, as well as a physical and financial investment, in their homes.) The response was typical not-in-my-backyard-ism, the NIMBY effect…with the fillip that the Habitat property at one time really was a neighbor's backyard. The land had been part of a family farm, and the neighbor had no desire to see his childhood playground turned into a building site.

He sued the Newtown zoning commission to block the project. The legal argument was shaky, but that hardly mattered, for Housatonic Habitat felt the pressure instantly. Being named in a lawsuit was bad enough – *hey, this organization's supposed to bring people together!* – but even worse, the affiliate had little choice but to plow ahead. Housatonic Habitat owned no other property, had none in the pipeline: Newtown was the only possible build site, and if it gave up on this one, the affiliate couldn't raise funds and would likely go dormant, perhaps forever. So the board settled the case (major concession: two houses, not three), on terms that still rankle. "The suit was totally frivolous," says long-time board member Colleen O'Rourke, "but we were being nice guys: 'Sure, wipe your feet on us!' We should've fought to the bitter end – hung that guy's balls out to dry, in plain English."

The room was silent when Larry finished. Roger broke the hush with a steely anger. "We have to get those site revisions," he said. "If we pay for it, we pay for it. This fellow, this surveyor, has to be told this is a major, major crisis discussed by the board. I'm quite weary of telling people every Sunday 'No, sorry, we're not building yet.'" Everyone knew what Roger was talking about: he'd lobbied his church, St. Stephen's Episcopal of Ridgefield, to sponsor the Newtown home with a $50,000 donation.

Christie Davey, the affiliate's president, attempted to lighten the mood. "We have to remember," she said, "that the engineering on this has been much more complex than anyone anticipated." She suggested the affiliate contact Habitat's Care-A-Vanners group, a collection of 'gypsy' volunteers who travel to Habitat build sites around the country; or institute a partial "blitz build," in which volunteers work intensely to complete one or more houses in a week or two. But the building-savvy around the table remained skeptical. "It'll be a miracle" if the house was finished by Thanksgiving, said Peter, the architect. Added Larry, "We don't want to kill the volunteers, do we?" Christie, a partner in an ad-sales company, concluded the discussion with "It's going to be challenging, the next couple months."

But Roger (photo, below right) wasn't done. "We have to understand," he continued, raising his voice, "that the word out there is, 'Housatonic Habitat can't build.' And it's tough to hear that we're hostage to this, or that, or the other thing. I don't want to depress everyone – we're all doing our very best, good-hearted people and all that – but I have to tell you I received a phone call the other day, from the pastor at one of our covenant churches, saying we were in trouble there.

Some of its volunteers have worked with Bridgeport Habitat as well, and apparently they've heard things like 'What are you dealing with Housatonic for? They don't build houses, all they have is lawsuits!' If that's the perception we're dealing with...well, frankly, after what I've heard tonight, I don't know how to respond."

The directors were stunned...not least because there was some truth to the characterization. Housatonic Habitat's ledger did in fact carry more lawsuits than finished homes – the Newtown dispute was the second court action, for a Danbury woman had filed a slip-and-fall claim after tripping on a sidewalk in front of the Elm Street house. But shouldn't Bridgeport Habitat cut its "little sister" some slack? Show compassion for the affiliate's troubles in bringing the Mickey Rooney-like, let's-build-a-house-together idea to Danbury? Where land was far more expensive, poverty hidden away, and affordable housing almost non-existent? Bridgeport should be *helping* Housatonic, not undermining it!

"Not very Christian of them," said Christie. "Boy," added Larry, equally upset, "I bet we're doing more site work in Newtown than they do on all their lots put together."

Site work – that was the big problem, but not the only one. John Kukulka, Housatonic Habitat's Construction Manager, would tick them off for me.

"If site development costs you $30,000," John said, "that's the real cost of the land – it's not a 'donation' at all. If a town's serious about affordable housing, they should give us some kind of break." And the house was 'overdesigned,' in order to fit in with neighboring homes. The foundation was L-shaped, John pointed out, rather than rectangular: every jog increased the chances of a concrete-pouring error, a framing mistake. The foundation was bi-level, too: the ground sloped, so while the east side of the house had two stories, the west side had three, if you counted the walk-in basement. (In most homes the basement would be the garage, but Habitat proscribes garages – another born-in-the-South legacy.) And the windows – they were everywhere, and appropriate for the pastoral setting...but each needed framing. For another client he might have recommended a picture window, which costs less than multiple double-hungs due to simpler framing and lack of hardware...but Habitat also prohibits picture windows, for sending the wrong message.

"We can't have all this fenestration," John said. "We've got to get away from this creeping affluence – our immediate reaction of 'You've got to have two bathrooms, right?' Well, you *don't*. The tract houses of Levittown – those were good houses, they had only one bathroom."

Site work, detailing, extra windows and extra space: all the things that made the project attractive to Newtown officialdom made the affiliate's 'affordable' house unaffordable to build. The affiliate was proud of its first "suburban" project, and the Jeffrey family was thrilled to live there...but the house, at the closing, was appraised at $225,000. Housatonic Habitat seemed to be building homes for the middle class.

John, who became involved with Housatonic Habitat a year after it acquired the Newtown lot, drove past the property one day while delivering his son to a soccer tournament. *Somebody's actually developing that?* he recalls thinking. *Man, I feel sorry for those guys.*

Four

"Not Charity but Capital"

One of the ironies of the Koinonia/Habitat story – many would call it fate, or God's will – is that Fuller (examining farm soil, right) arrived near the farm's nadir. A handful of people still lived there, and it retained an impressive roster of supporters, but in 1965 Koinonia Farm was no longer the *koinonia* Jordan envisioned. Some stalwarts had left out of dissatisfaction, often with Jordan's management style; others had moved away to start satellite communities, in Comer, Georgia, and in Neshanic, New Jersey. And as the civil-rights movement took hold, Koinonia came to be regarded less as a model community than an old-time spa, a rest stop for activists planning marches in Montgomery, Albany, Selma. Time, in short, was passing Koinonia by – not least because small-farm consolidation, and Sumter County's shift toward industry, was making agricultural life seem inconsequential.

Jordan himself had concluded that "the community of work is not possible" even for committed Christians. He strove for unanimity, but in due course conceded that work could not be assigned, talent gauged, authority apportioned, in a single, correct way, even with biblical guidance. (Every Habitat crew leader, sooner or later, comes to the same conclusion.) Jordan would have understood, and sympathized with, both the multicultural and what-would-Jesus-do ethics of the 1990's, but knew from experience how high-concept theories stumble when translated into practice. Reality – not to mention its countless strong-willed, self-confident, never-a-doubt interpreters – got in the way, rendering cloudy a seemingly transparent process.

Despite its lofty humanitarian goals, Koinonia Farm proved too single-minded, too hothouse-flower, to thrive. How could it be otherwise, when it managed to attract exactly two black partners over two decades – the very people the community was founded to serve? It's no surprise Jordan considered liquidating the farm in 1962, and lived at Koinonia until his death mainly because he couldn't get rid of it. He tried to pass it on, gratis, to other non-profit organizations, but even then had no takers.

Stuck in south Georgia, Jordan and his few remaining partners restructured Koinonia twice in the 1960's. The common purse was eliminated, craft industries were emphasized over agriculture, resident families became responsible for producing their own income. But the farm still seemed beyond saving, for Clarence Jordan was worn out, had fought too many unwinnable battles. The farm had made more enemies, locally, than friends; in ten years had gone from far ahead of the socio-political curve to well behind it. Jordan was reluctant to call Koinonia a failure, since it had blazed a trail for the civil-rights movement, but didn't want his "demonstration plot for the Kingdom of God" becoming a downscale bed-and-breakfast, a rest stop on the road to freedom.

The fall was steep, for in the 1950's Koinonia was at times a vibrant place, doing some of its most imaginative, resourceful work when literally under the gun. Anyone familiar with the farm (some work-

ers and partners show at left, in an undated photograph from the era) knew its social policies were progressive, but its agricultural know-how was as well, because Jordan wasn't hindered by tradition. A poultry major in college, he shared his expertise with anyone who'd listen. Chicken farming spread throughout Sumter County after Jordan introduced egg- and chicken-production; passers-by looked on admiringly when Jordan hitched his tractor to a mobile peanut-harvester of his own design. After Koinonia doubled in size, to 1100 acres, partners talked as if growth was inevitable, that building homes for residents was only a few years down the road.

The increasing acreage, the growing population, seemed healthy... but papered over, and perhaps accentuated, the fact that Koinonians were tolerated in Georgia but not accepted. Although a major goal of the farm was to break down the barriers of segregation, demonstrate its intrinsic flaws and social evils, Koinonia was itself segregated from the larger community. A few neighbors admired the farm for instituting a "cow library" from which poor families could borrow, free, a milk cow: but more resented the program as a "giveaway," a Trojan horse calculated to indoctrinate people into socialism, communism, and worse. Economic concerns, as always, trumped notions of fairness, with advances by one group presumed damaging to another.

The first major rupture with the locals occurred in 1950. Jordan, his wife Florence, and four other Koinonians were excommunicated from the Rehoboth Baptist Church for "advocating views and practices contrary to those of other members" – namely, having "brought people of other races" to church services. But there were many additional offenses: the Koinonians, the deacons wrote in their withdrawal-of-fellowship letter, "do constantly visit Negro churches in the community, and have persisted in holding services where both white and colored attend together"; and "disrupted the Christian unity and spirit which had previously prevailed." For such conduct – and for alleging, as Jordan undoubtedly did, that the church "possibly operated under False doctrines" – the Koinonians were struck from the church rolls.

Jordan, defrocked in neighbors' eyes, became a moving target. And the temper of the times was right for pariah-making, as the nation was being told to see enemies everywhere, even – especially – in their own backyards. Senator Joe McCarthy (photo at right) found Communists under every rock; halfway around the world, black South Africans were rioting against apartheid. Koinonia might claim only to "incarnate" the words of Jesus, but locals saw a Red collective, a dangerous cell dedicated to racial equality, pacifism, and socialism. Jordan, in other words, was a poster boy for un-Americanism, and thousands of Georgians wished him out of business (and out-of-state) permanently.

Destroying Koinonia would not, however, be easy. Jordan was sincere about living "according to the gospel"...and if that led to his death, well, Jesus showed the way. At times, indeed, Jordan seemed to seek martyrdom, going well beyond avenging-preacher mode; his sincerity was both strength and weakness.

Jordan's aw-shucks manner could seem glib, his devotion to principle holier-than-thou, especially when he spoke from the pulpit in avenging-preacher mode – young Grump again, spoiling for a fight, throwing gasoline on flames when the audience expected water. Listeners were alarmed when Jordan quoted the Bible's "give unto every man according as he has need," but when he said a Christian who'd never been called a Communist "wasn't worth his salt," they fumed. And when Jordan claimed most people not only couldn't differentiate between Jesus Christ and Karl Marx but "didn't know anything about either one of them"; when he thundered that the Christian church had "gone a-whoring" by spending small fortunes on fountains while parishioners used outhouses; well, he'd gone beyond the pale. (He also liked to say of Christianity, "We've got a body of ideas here that the Marxists can't hold a candle to. No one can.") Hoping to open eyes, he often closed ears.

The violence at Koinonia started in 1954, after the U.S. Supreme Court handed down the desegregation decision *Brown v. Board of Education*. The farm suddenly became much more threatening, an outpost of Yankee thinking – especially when Jordan agreed, in

May 1956, to sponsor two black students hoping to enroll at the business school of his alma mater. It was a courageous choice: blacks were supposed to know their place (as a white jury suggested the previous year when it acquitted two Mississippi men of murdering 14-year-old Emmett Till (shown at left) because he seemed to flirt with a white woman). Koinonia went from suspicious to dangerous, and for the next year the farm was under siege. Sugar was poured into gas tanks; shots were fired into the farm's roadside ham market, which was destroyed by a bomb blast soon after. Locals instituted a boycott, refusing all commerce or trade with Koinonia; it was difficult to get fuel, let alone seed or fertilizer. The district attorney of Sumter County even told the *Albany Journal* "Maybe what we need right now is for the right kind of Klan to stand up and use the buggy whip on some of these race mixers.... I had rather see my little boy dead than sit beside a nigra in the public schools."

But 1957 brought worse. The attacks became personal: shots were fired into Koinonia homes, one narrowly missing Jordan's daughter Eleanor. Buildings were burned at the farm and in the front yards of local blacks: they feared for their lives, and stayed clear of Koinonia. In an Associated Press story on the boycott, the sheriff was quoted as saying, "The people have had it up to here. We get reports of whites and Negroes strolling down the street together in Americus. One report said a white girl and two Negro boys walked down the street all eating popcorn out of the same bag." The publisher of the local newspaper compared Koinonia to "a cancer on the community and we ought to get rid of it."

The farm appealed for help, and scores of people arrived to provide witness, at the very least. Among the sympathizers was activist Dorothy Day (photo at right), who wrote in the *Catholic Worker* of being "shot at for the first time in my life" on the day before Easter. At one-thirty in the morning, as Day and a Koinonia resident – who'd brought along an accordion to pass the time – sat in a station wagon, "a car slowed up as it passed and peppered the car with shot. We heard sounds of repeated shots – a regular gunfire, and we were too startled to duck our heads." Neither woman was injured...and they continued their watch.

The Ku Klux Klan, knowing local authorities wouldn't enforce the law, had a free hand. (In 1961 Martin Luther King, Jr., would spend a night in the Americus jail, and pronounce its sheriff "the meanest man in the world.") After staging a rally on Americus' Friendship Road, more than a hundred white-robed Klansmen drove to Koinonia to confront the farm's leader...but were told there was none, everyone at the farm being equal. A few months later an Americus feedstore that challenged the boycott was blown up with dynamite, leading the town's Chamber of Commerce to send a delegation to Koinonia asking the farm to "move and leave us in peace." Jimmy Carter, just out of the Navy and trying to build his farm-and-warehouse business, sold Koinonia seed peanuts when others wouldn't, but mostly stayed on the sidelines.

Koinonia did not move, of course, for every violent incident strengthened Jordan's resolve to bear witness to Christian hypocrisy. But his faith was tested, especially when 'night riders' fired shotguns at Koinonia children playing volleyball. Jordan wrote President Eisenhower asking for help...but received only hounding, for Eisenhower forwarded the letter to J. Edgar Hoover at the F.B.I. Within weeks Jordan

(pictured above at right, on courthouse steps) was speaking to a Sumter County grand jury – as a defendant, accused of staging the gunfire and arson and bombings (now a regular part of Koinonia life) to drum up support. No indictments were handed down, but the grand jury announced in its official findings that Koinonia's Christianity was "sheer window dressing." Oddly, though, the jurors couldn't decide what creed Koinonia was "fronting" for – wild-eyed Communism, or fraudulent capitalism.

Koinonia's brush with notoriety – the attacks and court case were written up in the *New York Times*, *Newsweek*, *Time*, and other national publications – temporarily helped the farm. But battle fatigue took its toll. Long-time residents left because they lost any sense of safety, or felt thwarted by the Jordans' increasing disengagement; because Koinonia failed to become more politically engaged, or less politically engaged. And they left because, as one veteran put it, "we are so busy with survival we don't have time to minister." The Klan, to all intents and purposes, had won. It had isolated Koinonia so completely that the farm barely functioned, communing only with itself and a model, now, for no one.

The farm's major failure, in Jordan's view, was its inability to mobilize local blacks. Threats from the Klan obviously discouraged participation -- many blacks declined to work at Koinonia, fearing retribution – but farm policy was also to blame. Joining Koinonia essentially meant taking a vow of poverty, since it focused more on sharing wealth than making more, and for many whites -- often from northern states, with successful careers and decades of 'good living' behind them – such downward mobility was spiritually refreshing. (A partner once threatened to leave the farm because it acquired a television.) But giving up hard-won material goods in favor of joint ownership, for sharecroppers of any race, had little appeal. It didn't seem like progress: why abandon the American dream just when the country seemed willing, however grudgingly, to share its bounties?

By the early 1960's Jordan had accepted, at some level, that Koinonia was a "white" vision. The problem didn't lie in the message – of that he was sure – but might have something to do with the messenger, or the process of communication itself. Being a man of faith, Jordan wasn't easy prey for doubt, but in a deconstructionist age it's easy to imagine him thinking *I grew up white, privileged, and relatively wealthy, don't mind a good argument. Maybe I saw things a certain way, could've kicked ideas around a bit more? Read less, talked less, listened a bit more, and a bit more closely....*

Millard Fuller, when he drove up in 1965, was the answer to that unspoken prayer (even if his car was a Continental). He wasn't just new blood, full of energy and enthusiasm: he had brains, too, and the marketing experience, the business savvy, that Jordan conspicuously lacked. He could talk to people, moreover, without the intellectual paraphernalia, the know-it-all manner, the holier-than-thou moralism, that regularly marked Jordan's speech. Fuller (pictured, right, in 1969) could present Koinonia in a different light, illustrate its tolerance and diversity and principles without raising hackles, without explicitly challenging current practices. And he could also give Jordan time to think more deeply about another, more lasting problem, one that transcended Koinonia. *How, in this car-crazy, hero-killing, television-*

watching, soul-deadened, give-me-mine-now era, do you make Jesus Christ relevant?

Jordan (below, at his typewriter in 1961) would have time, at long last, to ponder not the back forty and the failing septic system, not management and mediation, but a better way to tell Jesus' story. It wouldn't be a cut-and-paste job, like Thomas Jefferson's expurgated, unreligious Bible (published after his death); it would be a startlingly new rendition, one the average farmer could relate to his own life. Two years earlier, preparing a speech for a Baptist convention, Jordan had found his model after noticing the parallels between the Bible's Ephesus, the city to which the Apostle Paul wrote about tolerance, and Birmingham, Alabama, from whose jail Martin Luther King, Jr., wrote his own famous letter in 1963. Jordan retitled Paul's missive "The Letter to the Christians in Birmingham," and with this voice spoke plainly of Koinonia's trials. The talk was greeted warmly, and Jordan knew he was in the translation business.

Jordan would work on his New Testament translations for the remainder of his life. There is nothing else like them, for Jordan was unintimidated by his material: written today, his *Cotton Patch Gospel* could be called *Jesus for Dummies.* He knew his Greek better than most translators, but more importantly, wrote with a particular audience in mind – the downtrodden, the ill-educated, the poor. College graduates, high-school graduates, understood Bible basics: but what about the illiterate? People who couldn't point to Israel or Palestine on the map, who didn't know what a manger was, or myrrh, or money-changing? *Now, what if Jesus were born in Gainesville, got baptized in the Chattahoochee, talked about 'splinters' instead of 'motes,' about 'fallen skunks' instead of 'ye cursed'? Said 'Howdy,' acted like a regular guy, except maybe for turning water into moonshine? Sure, a Jesus like that might upset a few people, but might make sense to thousands more....*

What Jordan wanted to do, writes Dallas Lee, was "recapture the ideas of the New Testament in a contemporary context that would make people feel like participants, not spectators." Or in Jordan's saltier words, he wanted to "help cotton-picking Christians understand what their pea-picking preachers had been saying." Clarence, by this time, was thoroughly disgusted with a good portion of the clergy, considering them too removed from Joe Citizen. "We want Paul's letters to have the simplicity, the earthiness which they had before Christians erected temples of mortar and stone," he wrote, using the word "temples" quite pointedly. How could men build magnificent shrines to an abstract power they had never actually seen, he asked, while their neighbors, whom they saw every day, went without? The seeds of Habitat went down deeply in Jordan's soul.

Millard Fuller was profoundly impressed by Jordan and Koinonia. But he had his marriage to think about, some personal reservations... and wasn't finished with New York City. The Manhattan pastor who counseled the Fullers after their separation was a trustee of Mississippi's Tougaloo College, and the school was about to launch a fund-raising campaign. Wasn't Fuller just the man for the job? The former millionaire wasn't entirely convinced, but since the pastor was making a reasonable suggestion to a re-born Christian, and Fuller had rejected his past but hadn't figured out his future, he agreed to take the position. Fuller spent the next two years setting up a New York development office and traveling the country speaking on Tougaloo's behalf.

The position seemed a good fit with Fuller's new world view. Tougaloo and Koinonia aspired to the same thing – getting past racial prejudice, giving the disadvantaged an opportunity, and the skills, with which to improve their lives. The job was not, however, the answer to Fuller's prayers. Within a few months he'd taken a leave of absence to spend eight weeks in Africa on a fact-finding tour for the United Church of Christ (with which Tougaloo was affiliated). The tour, in many ways, was penance. Church officials in Montgomery had asked Fuller to make the same trip two years earlier, but he had declined, saying it was "too expensive" in terms of lost business for Fuller & Dees.

The African trip would play a seminal role in the formation of Habitat for Humanity. The Fullers – Linda accompanied Millard, for the last thirty-odd years they've traveled together whenever possible – saw up close the depth of world poverty and the gulf between the haves and the have-nots. They also began to appreciate the connection between the two – that economic colonialism still existed, that a gain in the First World often entailed a loss in the Third. In one Mbandaka, a city of 150,000 in northern Zaire (now the Congo, again), they drove down streets lined with pitiful mud shacks housing thousands of recent arrivals. The hovels' occupants had left distant villages in hopes of work, because the new, native-run government had repealed the internal-movement laws of the Belgian era...but the Zairois administration, inexperienced and divided, was unprepared for the crowding masses. Millions of natives had benefited from colonial systems – safer water, better health care, higher productivity – but the improvements were transplants nonetheless, impositions born of conquest. These new vital organs worked...but they were never fully accepted, and subject to sudden rejection.

Fuller knew his work for Tougaloo was necessary and important, but soon found himself unfulfilled, unchallenged. Throughout adulthood he'd been his own boss, set the agenda for others to follow, but here he was filing expense sheets, writing never-to-be-looked-at reports, justifying his actions to managers and directors. Was that why he identified, after Linda left him, with post-colonial Africans and American blacks – because he suddenly knew, if only for a few days, the grief and lethargy of powerlessness? Of being forced to adapt to an existing system, one you didn't create, couldn't alter? Fuller had readily accommodated himself, years earlier, to American business culture, but only after leaving did he appreciate that it had required the ultimate sacrifice – the destruction of his inner self.

After nearly two years with Tougaloo, Fuller has written, he "felt pulled toward some kind of radical, dynamic Christian action." He was tired of *seeing* the world's problems and then, home again, *talking* about them: he wanted to act...which naturally led him back to Clarence Jordan.

His desire to serve the Lord was absolutely genuine, but boundless, too. Tougaloo simply could not contain him: Millard wanted to spread Jesus' words faster, deeper, and more effectively...which meant, essentially, in his own way. And that was largely Jordan's way, too, for although highly articulate, and a translator of the Bible, Jordan always thought actions spoke louder than words, that words without action were form without content. The only true word was God's, and you needed to experience it personally, understand it honestly, on your own. Fuller took that message to heart. *He's the real boss,* Fuller told himself, *the only boss, the President, Captain, CEO. And if I can do His work faster and better, more efficiently and more widely, on my own, in another way, in a new way... well, isn't that my Christian duty?* Integrated farming, living like Jesus, was well and good, but Fuller had bigger fish to fry.

Home-building, in early 1968, wasn't on Koinonia's radar screen. And it wasn't a particular interest of Jordan, who preferred lecturing at colleges and working on his Bible translations, or of Fuller, tying up loose ends at Tougaloo and puzzling over his next challenge. All Fuller knew, at this point, was that he couldn't get Koinonia out of his head, or heart. *People not just quoting the Gospel, but living it every day! As latter-day disciples, spreading the Word through deeds, getting something done, leaving the world better!* Fuller wrote to Jordan asking, with a certain desperation, "what do you have up your sleeve for me?" Jordan, always glad to hear from the energetic Fuller, replied, "Maybe God has something up His sleeve for both of us."

They met the following weekend, in May 1968, at a church in Atlanta. And one word kept coming up: *partnership.* Koinonia Farm was founded on that ideal, of course, but this new project – however realized – would be fashioned after a different model, defined more broadly, because both men had seen previous partnerships – Fuller's marriage, Jordan's "demonstration plot" – damaged by overconfidence and impatience, narcissism and narrow-mindedness. A true partnership explores divergent views, finds common ground, constantly remakes itself; never forgets that a vision can be selfish as well as selfless, and everything in-between. Jordan and Fuller called a meeting, hoping friends and colleagues and long-time supporters would see the merit in their inchoate, shapeless, but hopefully world-improving concept – that Koinonia's underlying principles could be resurrected in a form both contemporary and timeless.

Twenty people gathered at Koinonia three months later. And from their discussions one central idea emerged, an idea that Jordan, in his commitment to racial and economic justice, to books and words, had overlooked: that a *koinonia,* above all, was a state of mind. People tend to ignore abstractions until they're manifested in the real world: that's human nature, and why Jordan put the New Testament in "Southern-ese." And God did the same, at bottom, by "inventing" Jesus. By literally bringing the divine down to earth, by embodying Godhead, incarnating him, God allowed humans to feel, identify, to *act* like him – and not Him, a Being so far above and beyond the human plane as to be unreal, out-of-mind. Jesus was God-made-flesh in order to narrow the gap between the human and the heavenly, to show that man could live on a better, higher, more selfless existence.

Jordan, at some point, must have understood that Koinonia Farm was too much too soon, too look-at-me, too in-your-face; too much about Jordan, and not enough about Jesus. It was too much *tell* and not enough *show*; forced its way into living rooms saying 'Pay attention!' instead of tapping at kitchen doors and offering a cup of coffee. So what should the next generation of Koinonians do, with the second chance offered by Fuller's return? They were a terrific team, Fuller and Jordan, greater than the sum of their parts…and together, perhaps, could instigate a more 'natural' community, an organic koinonia that evolved in its own way, that wasn't plastered, limited, by its founders' fingerprints. The community would still be tied together by Christian values, of course, and by common purpose, but it would speak a universal language, some cultural equivalent of Esperanto.

Fuller knew what Jordan was getting at. As a lawyer, he'd long since grasped that the best way to win an argument was to frame it as a syllogism, to persuade listeners to accept a seemingly benign proposition and then lead them, step by inexorable step, to a conclusion they might have rejected moments before. You don't convert people by saying, "Hello, I have The Answer, the One Way!"; you don't correct injustice by saying, "I'm taking over, because you're a bunch of idiots!"; you don't correct a situation by saying, "Stand aside, you're doing it all wrong!" You lead – convert, correct, improve -- by example: by living the life you believe in, by walking your talk…which is, of course, the story of Jesus' days on earth. Koinonia Farm grew from this same Biblical "mustard seed" of faith, but the soil of Habitat for Humanity proved far more fertile.

A story from these post-Koinonia, pre-Habitat years captures the problematic nature of Jordan's mission, and of his personality, too.

He and Fuller stayed with an Atlanta pastor during the weekend they grappled with Koinonia's future, and one day the pastor asked for advice on a personnel issue. The church's janitor worked seven days a week for $80, but the pastor – who had already insisted the church raise the janitor's pay by $30 a week – knew the man, who had eight children and a twenty-mile commute, was still grossly underpaid.

The pastor, apparently unfamiliar with Jordan's radical views, asked for advice. Jordan inquired about the pastor's own life – two children, house down the street, decent income – and said, "Well, why not just swap salaries with him? Surely you could live more easily on his salary than he can."

The white pastor "turned whiter," according to Fuller, and after some hemming and hawing, admitted that Jordan's suggestion was unassailable. Christian doctrine, taken literally, almost *required* the pastor to switch salaries; he had much, the janitor had the little, and the exchange would likely increase the total happiness of the two families. Perhaps the pastor did make the swap – Fuller never learned the outcome – but that's unlikely, for Jordan made the pastor feel foolish, selfish, unworthy. Jordan's righteousness, his desire to win arguments, could make his views easy to dismiss, for would a true Christian – a fellow preacher no less! – deliberately embarrass another?

Fuller tells this story with admiration, but it's difficult to imagine him challenging someone so personally. The challenges he issues today – to eliminate substandard housing worldwide, to take up the cause in one's own neighborhood or nation – aren't tinged with criticism or superiority. They do, however, track Jordan's deepest goals: to spread the word about Christian ideals. Clarence disdained the political world for the compromises, the distortions and deceptions, it entailed, but Millard would soon demonstrate how a more tolerant, less judgmental approach could achieve much more.

Within days of the May meeting the Fullers had moved to Koinonia to implement the 'partnership' idea. Would it be a school? A training program? A movement? No one knew: perhaps it would be all three, and something else besides. For advice Millard and Clarence contacted old friends, supporters, and like-minded acquaintances, and by the fall had assembled a group of philosophical and financial backers. (Four of the invitees were from Connecticut, in part because many Georgia blacks had moved to the capital, Hartford, in hopes of improving their lot.) "We've got to think big," as Jordan told supporters gathered for the 1968 meeting. "This is not a time for spiritual pygmies. We're living in a land of giants, and pygmies seldom have influence on giants. We're going to have to think in gigantic terms."

The Big Idea that emerged from the conference – the one that became a Big Reality – was something called the "Fund for Humanity." It was based, Jordan wrote in a fund-raising letter, on the premise that

> What the poor need is not charity but capital, not caseworkers but co-workers. And what the rich need is a wise, honorable and just way of divesting themselves of their overabundance.

It would be a mission allowing – imploring – people on opposite ends of the economic spectrum to help one another. You can hear Fuller's influence in the change of tone, in the suggestion that the wealthy, too, can be partners…although Jordan, once again, didn't know when to stop. He concluded the letter with a quote from St. Augustine (with whose writings Locke was quite familiar): "He who possesses a surplus possesses the goods of others." (The illustration of Augustine at left is from an 1885 book about the "hundred greatest men.") Jordan glosses the sentence as "a polite way of saying that anybody who has too much is a thief," but even that provocation didn't undermine the appealing symmetry of the Fund, a form of wealth redistribution that Pierre Proudhon himself ("property is theft") would have approved…but voluntary, legal, and hopefully infectious.

The Fund for Humanity was to have three major branches – Partnership Farming, Partnership Industries, and Partnership Housing, which tracked the basic human needs of food, clothing, and shelter. The first two programs, farming and small industry, were intended to be money-makers, financial support for the outreach work of Koinonia Partners (as it was thereafter called, and remains to this day). The Fund, considering Koinonia had abandoned field-crop farming years earlier and knew little about industry or home-building, was an enormous leap of faith. But Jordan was ready to jump, for he'd concluded, with Fuller's encouragement, that American capitalism could be modified to suit the farm's spiritual ends. Jordan was lit with true faith, but Fuller added mirrors to that flashlight beam, and installed it in a revolving lighthouse.

Instead of being a constant rebuke to American consumer culture, the Fund would redefine capitalistic success. Why should *getting* trump *giving* when Fuller knew, from experience, the me-first-and-always philosophy was a trap? Didn't the U.S. rise, quite explicitly, from Christian principles like "It is nobler to share than to get"? (That's Jordan's translation of Jesus' "It is more blessed to give than to receive," from a standard version of Acts: the cover of a modern reprint of the Cotton Patch *Luke and Acts* is shown at right.) The Fund would work something like a Tlingit potlatch, where giving was valued above all, profits measured in non-economic terms; where numerical measurements were presumed to be reductive, a defense against uncertainty, the unquantifiable. (Sanskrit scholar Heinrich Zimmer put the idea this way: "The best things in life cannot be told, and the second best are misunderstood.") Properly implemented, the Fund would eliminate bizarre, unproductive inequities in which the rich idler was paid not to grow tomatoes while the poor sharecropper worked from dawn to dusk...yet fell still deeper into debt. The example was not a metaphor: Jordan could name two such men, Sumter County residents and practically neighbors.

Land – Jordan and Fuller realized, walking squarely in the footsteps of Thomas Jefferson, that *land* was the biggest bottleneck to happiness, justice, godliness. How could the poor and uneducated advance, exercise their full rights as citizens, their dream as individuals, if they didn't have a decent place to live? A place where they could be themselves, feel safe, call their own? If the people who worked the land also owned it, they'd have an investment in society, a home to protect, a place to set down roots. Maybe Jordan had it backward: instead of asking people to give up material things in quest of a Christian life

– which Koinonia essentially required of partners – why not use material things as an incentive? Not just any material things, of course – meals were eaten and forgotten, shoes worn out and thrown away – but something permanent, a constant reminder of community, faith, interdependence. The Fund couldn't provide everyone in need with a Jeffersonian 50 acres, but a quarter-acre wasn't out of the question, especially if large land-owners – the equivalent of 18th-century French nobility, owning land for pleasure or investment, not social benefit – did their part.

But land, practically free for the taking in Jefferson's time, was growing expensive. Could the Fund do something about that? Yes: by applying what Fuller would call, years later, "the economics of Jesus" – the Bible's pronouncement that money loaned to the poor should carry no interest. The fund would not only refuse to charge interest payments but profit, too, so Jack Q. Poorfellow could become a homeowner for the equivalent of rent money. His modest mortgage payments, moreover, would be recycled: rather than buying boats and fine wines, sports cars and second homes, for those who profited handsomely from real-estate transactions, the payments would be put back into the Fund, for the purchase of more property to be sold, in turn, to other landless people.

Poetic justice, thought Jordan: *we'll make what goes around, come around.* The well-off and guilt-ridden, many of whom owned stock in companies that exploited the poor's lack of capital, would make amends by contributing to the Fund. By returning with one hand what they took with the other, they'd build an inheritance for the socially disinherited. The Fund would demonstrate that wealth redistribution is best accomplished by persuasion, not force, that a rich person's excess money had far more value as a poor person's monthly nut.

"I don't see any guarantee in this Partnership Movement that it won't be a fiasco," Jordan said. "But we sure can't make things any worse."

The Fund for Humanity's first solicitation letter, sent to some 12,000 people, generated only a few thousand dollars – not much, but enough to convince Jordan and Fuller that the idea was worth pursuing. They weren't waiting, however, for human validation; a few Koinonians had already started partnership farming alongside local blacks, and a contractor was laying out a 42-lot housing development on the farm's north side.

The homes would be simple, four-room structures with cement floors, concrete-block walls, and asphalt-shingle roofs. (The sign and structures at right date from 1979.) No, not much of a house – but far superior to the falling-down shacks in which sharecroppers typically lived, not least because Fund for Humanity homes had indoor plumbing, electricity, and a decent kitchen…all for a monthly mortgage of $25. Today, you won't see that sort of shack in Sumter County unless you travel to Archery, a community outside Plains, where museum-quality copies have been built to replicate the farm on which Jimmy Carter grew up. The real shacks have disappeared – largely because the local Habitat affiliate, pushed by one of Fuller's many "challenge" programs, by the year 2000 had offered every willing, poorly housed county resident the chance to build and purchase their own Habitat home. In Sumter County, at least, Fuller's dream has been realized.

Jordan died in October 1969, weeks before the first partnership house was completed. Frank Jordan Sr. said his brother "died of a broken heart," but that's only half right: yes, his heart gave out, but Dallas Lee writes that Koinonia's founder, in his final weeks, was "pleased and more relaxed than he'd been in years." Fuller had taken a major weight off his shoulders, set the farm in a promising new direction, and put it on decent financial footing, so Jordan was happy to sit in his writing shack in the pecan orchard and work on his "Cotton Patch" translation of the Gospel according to John. He was full of faith once more…though never imagined he'd fathered an organization that would give new meaning to volunteerism all over the world, or a Bible translation that would become an off-Broadway musical and a staple of community theater. Jordan's legacy only became apparent decades after his death.

He was buried in a coffin-shipping container – some accounts say a refrigerator box -- in an unmarked grave on Koinonia's Picnic Hill.

Jordan didn't want a memorial, or a casket, and would have laughed uproariously at Fuller's having to drive into town in the farm's station wagon, his mentor's corpse in the back seat, because the coroner refused to pick up the body. Friends, partners, and relatives gathered for a funeral ceremony the next day, at which Fuller read a newly translated passage from Jordan's final work. "Don't love the old order," John proclaims after Jesus' crucifixion. "If anyone loves the old order, it is not the Father's love that's in him. For everything that's in the old order – the hankering for physical comforts, the hankering for material things, the emphasis on status – is not from the Father but is from the old order itself."

As friends dropped red Georgia clay on the recycled cedar box, two-year-old Faith Fuller broke into the only song she knew: "Happy Birthday."

Five

"...But We're Gonna Be Busy"

Few cities have fallen as far, and as fast, as Bridgeport, Connecticut. At the end of World War I, it was considered the industrial capital of the United States, was going to be the kind of "workers' paradise" that Marx could only dream about. The Locomobile was built in Bridgeport, making the city, very briefly, the automobile capital of the U.S. (its factory had one last hurrah when Buckminster Fuller built his sea-slug-shaped Dymaxion car there in 1933). Also manufactured in the city were Singer sewing machines, Underwood typewriters, Eaton valves, Raybestos brakes, General Electric appliances, Columbia phonograph records, Warner corsets, Remington ammunition, and myriad other industrial and consumer products. As late as 1938 – a decade after the founding of Sikorsky Aviation in neighboring Stratford – Bridgeport was called the most diversified manufacturing city in the nation, a resilient town because some industries were sure to thrive when others hit the skids.

But it didn't turn out that way. The first American city to bet its future on the Industrial Age, Bridgeport was likewise the first to experience wholesale de-industrialization. With old and inefficient factories, high wages, and worker-friendly politics – for decades it was governed by a Socialist mayor, Jasper McLevy, who was inspired by Edward Bellamy's utopian novel *Looking Backward* – by the 1970's the city couldn't compete with Japanese manufacturers, offshore producers, and non-union workers in the South and Midwest. Although a few defense-related industries remain in the area, Sikorsky prominent among them, most moved to greener pastures. Unemployment rose; the immigrants, who traditionally manned the factories, kept coming; and then, in the 1980's, crack cocaine arrived. Crime skyrocketed, the city earned the nickname "Deathport," and in 1991 Bridgeport became the first major city in the U.S. to declare municipal bankruptcy. Or tried to, at least; it even failed at failing, for a judge refused to approve the city's legal claim.

The city's industrial lineage is memorably captured in the Remington Arms shot tower (right), the tallest structure in Connecticut (165 feet) when completed in 1909. It's a red-brick, stone-trimmed, birthday-cake of a building that shows the civic-mindedness of Marcellus Hartley Dodge, Remington's CEO: not only did he insist on an attractive tower, but paid for it personally, not wanting to put the company at risk. Ten tons of lead were melted in twin cauldrons at the top of the tower, then mixed with antimony and arsenic; the mixture was poured through metal sieves to create, as the droplets spun in their fall to cooling water vats, symmetrical pellets. At its peak the shot tower produced a billion shot-pellets a day, and operated even into the 1980's, making weights for helicopter rotors.

Remington Arms was once the gem in Bridgeport's tiara, but all that's left, today, is an empty setting. The company's Boston Avenue plant – a long stone's throw from the shot tower – was once the single largest factory in the U.S.: a half-mile long and covering nearly 80 acres, its workers produced up to 5,000 rifles a day for Czar Nicholas II during the Great War (making for a total of one million). (Remington happily sold arms to the Kaiser as well, at least until the U.S. declared war on Germany in 1917.) The Barnum Avenue property, home to the shot tower, covers 60 acres, and is overseen by the tower's last manager. "You could clean up and use it tomorrow," says Gary Hayduk, one of many Hayduks who spent 150 years, collectively, with Remington.

Hayduk took me up the tower one morning, and when I tugged on a leather-loop pulley belt connected to a shot-sorting table – only perfectly round pellets rolled into collection bins – it was still taut.

The Bridgeport Habitat warehouse stands in the shadow of the shot tower. The affiliate had more than an acre of floorspace in the Remington complex, and can expand almost indefinitely because the buildings here – brick, a century old, with fifty-foot ceilings – are practically worthless. The place is a giant brownfield, carrying traces of arsenic, lead, asbestos, and many other toxic materials (the floor is full of ground-in brass cartridges), but Bridgeport Habitat volunteers don't care. Mostly retirees, they're in the warehouse only a few hours a week, and beyond self-centered thinking. Health risks? They'd rather die with their work boots on.

I'm working in Bridgeport because Housatonic Habitat's troubles in Newtown caused some soul-searching. A management consultant joined the Housatonic board, and the result was a strategic plan intended to create sound organizational principles to go along with the affiliate's do-good instincts. Some board members were deeply opposed to the plan, fearing a loss of emotional connection. "We're called Habitat for *Humanity*," said Colleen. "I can see it coming – it'll become project-to-project, e-mail-to-e-mail, instead of person-to-person."

I was intrigued, however, not least because the plan's fact-finding requirements allowed me to see if Bridgeport Habitat was, in fact, part of Housatonic Habitat's problem. To a degree it was: the founding director of Habitat for Humanity of Greater Bridgeport (its official name) told me point blank that Housatonic Habitat was screwing up, implying the Danbury group was a suburban feel-good project that drained resources from affiliates that helped the truly poor rather than the lower-middle-class. Bridgeport Habitat did exactly what Millard Fuller asked, she said, putting up homes with families who hoped for iron bathtubs "because that's where you put the children when the gunfire starts."

I sympathized, for the Bridgeport director's view was shared by many of Housatonic Habitat's own volunteers and board members. *If you're not building, you're not fulfilling the Habitat mission.* Months passed before I understood the counter-argument – that Habitat was at least as much about building relationships as building houses, that building relationships was part of the home-building process. To separate those elements went against Habitat's emphasis on partnership, especially when the director seemed to regard Housatonic as more competitor than ally, a drain on potential resources than a younger sibling to be helped, advised, nurtured…and in that sense, Bridgeport Habitat was falling down on the job, too.

I got the chance to see how Bridgeport Habitat had become so successful on the construction side (40 houses then, more than 100 as of this writing) when the affiliate gave a series of workshops on "best practice" Habitat home-building. Reading blueprints, framing walls, setting trusses, installing windows, nail-gunning shingles and siding: the idea was to turn regular Bridgeport volunteers into crew leaders, to eliminate "re-dos"…and I was allowed to sit in. The catch: attendees were expected to volunteer with Bridgeport one day a month -- which was fine by me, because Housatonic, at the time, wasn't building at all.

Bridgeport volunteers gather at the warehouse around 8 in the morning. The contrast with Housatonic Habitat couldn't be starker: while Danbury construction crews work out of a two-bay garage, half-filled with overstuffed cardboard boxes and an engine-less, grey-primed 1950's Chevy, Bridgeport's warehouse has hundreds of racks and cubbies, an entire room dedicated to power tools and supplies. I felt a wave of warehouse envy, and noted that the "scientific management" that once dominated Remington's productions lines – obsolete machine tools, from lathes and grinders to presses and drills, dotted the shop floor – was present here as well.

A bit like Noah's ark, I thought, surreptitiously examining the day's crew. Dark-skinned men and women – Dominican, Puerto Rican, Somali – putting in sweat-equity hours; neighborhood teenagers working toward voc-tech degrees; hired plumbers and electricians collecting fittings; Habitat staffers taking head counts, filling in forms, waiting for opportunities to interrupt. And then there's my contingent, the regular volunteers, who will intermingle with the other groups in the course of the day but right now are drinking coffee and shooting the breeze. In torn blue jeans, beat-up jackets, and faded t-shirts, we're the day-laborers of this scene, awaiting assignments and hoping to avoid everyone's least-favorite job – warehouse detail. I wonder: has a regular unknowingly worked on a home where his lawn-cutter or gardener will live? His stone-wall mason, his asphalt sealer?

The pool of regulars varies from day to day, week to week. On Mondays, my usual Bridgeport day, it's Allen, Frank, Ken, Linc, Fred, Mike, Lance, Phil, Ray, Ron, the Eds, the Bobs, a few others. (Mary, Margo, and Sherrie are regulars, too, but went directly to the Women's Build house, where the women do the heavy lifting and the men run the bake sales.) There's always catching up to do – someone's been traveling, or skiing, or visiting the grandkids – but the talk always turns to homes in progress. Bridgeport, most years, hopes to complete 15 homes, but right now it's way behind schedule. Of course.

"Guess we passed the inspection on Orchard, if they're sheetrocking tomorrow."

"When's the family supposed to move into Newfield? Be nice if it's before school starts."

"You seen Tom around? He's got my T bevel."

"Those modular homes on Pembroke – not as slick as they looked at first, huh?"

"Jeez – they're supposed to save time, right, but when you factor in the adjustments, the futzing around, you...."

"Hey Jim, what was that I saw in the paper – 18 lots in Stratford? Are they kidding?"

Jim Kirven, the construction supervisor, here five days a week and more, adjusts his Green Bay watch cap. "I don't know what's happening with that," he says. "But I know we're gonna be busy."

We're on Hanover today, a single-family burn-out with a distinguished lineage. The porch roof is held up with eight-inch, lathe-turned columns; the banister leading to the second floor is mahogany; the multiple, steep-pitched roofs go every which way, in the Victorian style, their shingles laid in complex patterns. *Fixed up in San Francisco, I think, this place'd go for a million-plus.*

The city of Bridgeport sold the property (similar to the four burn-outs or rot-outs on the previous page, but nicer) to Habitat for a dollar, anxious to return the property to the tax rolls. As usual, the affiliate first hoped for demolition, then considered rehabilitating the house as a duplex. The frontage proved too narrow for a second stairwell, though, and local building codes inflexible, so the building stayed as it was…most of it, at least. The house, according to Habitat guidelines, was too large even for a six-member family – the organization builds "simple, decent" housing, nothing more elaborate-- so the affiliate came up with a drastic, Solomonic solution. The back third of the house was amputated with power saws, torn down by a backhoe, and trucked to the city dump.

The structural rehabilitation, by this time, was nearly complete. The foundation was checked out, the ground floor supported with lally columns, the roof replaced; the interior walls – and the new rear wall – were framed. (Above, a nearly finished Bridgeport Habitat rehab.) But there's still plenty to be done even before we start the time-consuming interior work. A church-sponsored crew had started siding the back on the previous Saturday, working as high as the scaffolding allowed, and today we hope to finish the job. First, though, we had to sheath, insulate, and weather-proof the house's gable end, its peak perhaps 40 feet off the ground. And to get that high we'll use the affiliate's hydraulic lift – an old 'man-lift' once owned by the phone company.

Tom and Frank had already clambered into the lift bucket – to my surprise, because Tom claimed to be afraid of heights. A handful of volunteers have run the machine (that's Linc using it, on the opposite page), but Frank, recently retired from Sikorsky, is usually at the controls. A helicopter pilot, he has a natural feel for the manlift's twin joysticks, which allow the operator to turn, lift, and tilt the cherry-picker platform in any direction, and drive the base unit along the ground as well. Today, though, the base is recalcitrant, the ground wet from rain and the backyard chewed up with backhoe tracks.

"Shit," says Frank, under his breath, after twenty minutes of driving the base back and forth, back and forth, trying to maneuver between the Scylla of the giant dumpster and the Charybdis of a muddy spot. It's a rare curse from Frank; the lift, no longer a precision instrument, requires his full attention.

"Maybe we should call the auto club," says Fred, and everyone laughs. We're standing around, waiting, because there's nothing else to do; tool belts are on, extension cords run, cutting jigs set up, saws plugged in, the air-compressor charged. I've even sharpened my carpenter's pencil with a utility knife.

But Frank has found his path, is rolling, hardly even slows down as he approaches the house. We brace for collision – the rig's platform often lurches spastically when the controls are released – but Frank maneuvers within inches of the house. That's another reason I'm still on the ground: stand on third-floor scaffolding when it's suddenly bumped, and you won't forget the adrenaline rush as you paw for a safety rail. *If I'd been leaning down to pick up a prybar, or on tiptoe to drive one last inconvenient nail....*

Tom and Frank will be putting up roof-line flashing on the right side of the house. I'm partnered with Mario, installing plywood on the left side. Mario, a native Ecuadoran who's completed half of the required 500 sweat-equity hours for his own Habitat house, down the street, moves around the scaffolding like a cat: he practically jumps from platform to platform, brace to brace. Like many of Bridgeport homeowners-to-be, he's had more building experience than the typical volunteer. Angel, the affiliate's warehouse manager, helped build relatives' concrete-block homes as a youth in Puerto Rico, and I hear similar stories from Central American and Caribbean-born homeowners, who dominate the neighborhoods where Bridgeport Habitat works. ("I don't know why," Jim Kirven tells me at one point, "but we just don't get too many applications from the black community.") Mario is particularly experienced, for he once worked for a local construction company.

At first we make good progress, putting up the sheathing as squarely as possible and securing it to studs. We get into a rhythm: lift, place, level, nail. Our speed is partly a function of Mario's day-labor days, for he knows the best way to thread large sections of plywood through scaffold braces, how to drape a nail-gun hose over his shoulder so the tool falls readily to hand. But it's also due to his strength, because Mario, despite his small size, can handle four-by-eight plywood with ease.

We screech to a stop, though, on reaching the re-framed gable face. The surface isn't flat; some original lumber protrudes a half-inch past the new studs, and a few ancient fascia boards have yet to be removed. We end up paring down plywood with utility knives, building up studs with shims, decapitating hand-cut nails with a Sawzall (which lives up to its name). The nails, with their fat bodies and rectangular heads, drive home the age of the house (well over a hundred years) and the fact it was made by hand.

Allen Marx, who also dislikes heights, has been cutting plywood for us as well as siding for Margo and Jen, working on the front of the house. "Hey," he calls to the menfolk around noon, "what're you guys doing, watching? They're almost done in front!" We grin, knowing our chains are being pulled, and that Allen (photo right), a former commodities trader who will become Bridgeport Habitat's president the following year, is ready to eat. Just the core volunteers go: Mario has to get to his paying

job, and the women volunteers have brought their own lunches. We're grateful, because we don't have to lock up all the tools and hoses and equipment, which tend to disappear if unattended. Stolen tools are regularly offered back to

Habitat, very cheaply, a few days later...which is why every bit of equipment is branded with pink spray paint. The local pawn shop knows the mark, and calls the Habitat office whenever a nail-gun with a pink tattoo lands on the counter.

We finish the siding the following week. Now I'm the cutter, this time working in the huge attic, which must be eighteen feet at its highest point. (On the previous page, Bridgeport volunteers getting ready to cut.) Fred and Frank are on the man-lift, and in minutes I'm taking cut-calls from Fred – "Five-seven-and-three-quarters," "This one's notched -- three inches deep, 24 length, starting at thirty-four-and-five-eights." I measure the siding, put it on the straight-cut jig, run the blade, cut any needed notch, hand the section out the window. The siding, a cement-composite plank called Hardiboard, produces a nasty dust when cut, so I put on a mask.

"Don't you want the guillotine?" asks Frank, referring to a heavy-duty, hand-operated chopper that creates no dust at all. (A student uses one at right.) But I've never gotten a good, straight cut with the guillotine – either its blades are slack, or my technique is off – so I'm using a special, diamond-dust blade in a standard circular saw. A minor point, perhaps, but I appreciate Habitat's letting me work as I want to, with the tools I like; trusts, in short, my judgment. Trust: an amazing thing, really, looking back on my learning curve with the organization, my early mistakes...but then again, that's the core of Habitat, isn't it? Trusting people to do the right thing, to do their best? Though it's a standing joke among volunteers: *What're they gonna do, fire us? Dock our pay?* Working for nothing proves oddly empowering, we're as free as free agents get.

Intermission

Jordan's 'Bible for Beginners'

Clarence Jordan essentially retired from farm management after the Fullers moved to Koinonia in 1968. He still believed people could overcome prejudices, learn new ways of thinking, by working alongside one another, but had accepted that the farm's original concept was outdated. Small-farm agriculture was dying, American culture was growing violent, young people were rebelling, experimenting, seeking new ways and new spiritualities: Jordan thought his message was even more relevant to this new America, but couldn't devote himself to communicating it while simultaneously managing a farm. And agriculture, of course, was only one means to a far bigger end – a worldwide *koinonia*, a community based on sharing and equality, on love and understanding. Jordan, with Fuller's encouragement, returned to his greatest strength -- retailing provocative ideas in an engaging, down-home manner.

From the beginning Jordan had spoken about Koinonia Farm to anyone who asked, mostly congregations and college groups. But lecturing became a priority after the creation of the Fund for Humanity...and Jordan, like Fuller, was an exceptionally effective speaker. The audio tapes of his sermons can be mesmerizing, and are so effective it's difficult at times to fathom his relative obscurity today...until, that is, you look at the competition. Martin Luther King, Jr., Eldridge Cleaver, the Berrigan brothers, Barry Goldwater: Jordan could appear milquetoast by comparison, calling for neither bombs nor passive resistance but a Jesus-like faithfulness, and speaking not to cameras but small groups of sympathetic Christians. His critique of the American experiment was, at bottom, even more radical than those of his more famous peers, focusing very specifically on the shortcomings of modern capitalism...but his intellectual bent, Christian perspective, and mistrust of human authority (including his own) made him suspicious of the public spotlight. While activists toured the country preaching against Vietnam and prejudice and exploitation, Jordan would be alone in his pecan-orchard shack, thinking and writing and contemplating the word of God.

With Fuller running Koinonia, Jordan had time for a project he'd been kicking around since the early 1950's – producing a modern, accessible version of the New Testament. For sermons he'd always relied on his own translations of the Bible, because others, he thought, were fundamentally ineffective, and often inaccurate. *Grammatically accurate, maybe, but* turgid! *Philosophically opaque! So darn* dull! *The 'doeth's and 'spake's and 'begats,' the Pharisees and Ninevehs, the 'It is written's and 'Ye have heard's: who grasps the sense when they can't follow the words? Who catches the meaning when the sentence pushes the reader, the listener, away?*

Jordan's translation would be loose, measured by traditional, language-based standards. He would reach for the idea *behind* the words, would re-write and ignore, even transform passages to fit the New Testament's over-riding message. And he did so with enormous attention to detail, to etymological niceties, because he didn't want "some little jackleg preacher tying me up in knots because I didn't know what my Lord said." Jordan burned for people to know Jesus as well as he did, a man whose message was radical as well as redeeming...redeeming, indeed, because it was radical.

Jordan produced "Cotton Patch" translations of Paul's Epistles, the General Epistles, Acts, Hebrews, Luke, Matthew, and the first eight chapters of John. And they are startling even to 21st-century eyes, and even if Jordan considered the translations common-sensical. "Crucifixion" becomes "lynching"; "Jews" become "whites"; "Negroes" become "Gentiles"; "Pharisees" become "segregationists." Jordan knew these renditions would raise eyebrows, but each was linguistically defensible. "Pharisee," for example, in both Greek and Hebrew means "one who separates himself," so "segregationist" is a reasonable translation. ("If we translate [Pharisee] as it should be translated," Jordan noted wryly, "I think a lot of Southern Christians might join Buddhism or some other religion.") Jordan considered retaining "crucifixion," but thought modern crosses were "so shined, so polished, so respectable" that the symbol had lost its "original content of terrific emotion, of violence, of indignity and stigma, of defeat." And Jesus' death was more like a lynching than a court-ordered execution, in Jordan's view, because Pontius Pilate bowed to the mob's call for a killing, then washed his hands of the deed. Jordan also knew that so-called 'legal justice' is sometimes neither: in the South, he observed, "more people have been lynched 'by judicial action' than by unofficial ropes."

Jordan understood the ins-and-outs of Bible translation as well as anyone, but didn't want to miss the forest for the trees. (He had faced the same problem in farming, being far too detail-oriented to make a good manager.) "By stripping away the fancy language, the artificial piety, and the barriers of time and distance," Jordan wrote,

> this version puts Jesus and his people in the midst of our modern world, living where we live, talking as we talk, working, hurting, praying, bleeding, dying, conquering, alongside the rest of us. It seeks to restore the original feeling and excitement of the fast-breaking news – good news – rather than musty history.

Predictably, Jordan's translations caused offense in some quarters. "The author should be shot for making such a mockery of the Scriptures," wrote one reader, calling Jordan an "infidel" who would burn in hell – on a pyre, presumably, of his own books. (Of the Cotton Patch "Paul's Epistles" a critic on Amazon.com has volunteered, "In my opinion it is a very huge mockery of Christ and his life and doings here on earth. I have not personally read the book, but i [sic] have heard about it.") Jordan's publisher – Association Press, an arm of the YMCA – had its own difficulties with the translation, substituting "genitals" where Jordan used "penis." Showing a language maven's regard for specificity, Jordan argued that the word "has no vulgar connotations" and would shock only people who "think of Jesus as a eunuch"...but in those pre-Bobbit, pre-Clinton, pre-Snoop Dog days, he was obliged to accept the bowdlerization.

Jordan's Jesus was born to a woman named Mary and her fiancé, Joseph Davidson, in Gainesville, Georgia. Herod, the Governor, heard rumors that a baby with that name would grow up to take his place, and ordered Jesus killed; but an angel sent by the Lord told Joseph to "Get moving, and take your wife and baby and highball it to Mexico."

The family did, living there until Herod died and the angel returned to say (still with a drawl) that they should go to Valdosta, Georgia. Jesus learned the Bible backwards and forwards, and as an adult encountered John the Baptizer ("dressed in blue jeans and a leather jacket…living on corn bread and collard greens"), who baptized him in the Chattahoochee River. Jesus, soon after, started the "God Movement," telling followers he would travel to Atlanta and "go through terrible things at the hands of the leading church people."

Jesus' journey from cradle to cross remains, in Jordan's hands, The Greatest Story Ever Told (or as Jordan's followers say, Re-Told). And it's arguably improved, too, because Jordan not only made the story "flow" better, with his Southerner's knack for tale-telling, but focused on the meaning of Jesus' life rather than his words. He didn't forget, moreover, that the New Testament was intended to change behavior, not just beliefs. Jordan thought Jesus' life pretty much spoke for itself, and the more he could bring that life "to life," the more effective that life – and death – would be.

Jesus' story is cleaner in Georgia, less cluttered, than in the King James Version of the Bible. Matthew 6:16-18, for example, is rendered in the KJV Bible as:

> Moreover when ye fast, be not, as the hypocrites, of a sad countenance: for they disfigure their faces, that they may appear unto men to fast. Verily I say unto you, They have their reward.
>
> But thou, when thou fastest, anoint thine head, and wash thy face;
>
> That thou appear not unto men to fast, but unto thy Father which is in secret: and thy Father, which seeth in secret, shall reward thee openly.

Jordan's version, by contrast, reads as follows:

> Now when you go to church, don't be like the religious phonies who put on a solemn face to impress men with their piety. Rather, when you go to church, act perfectly normal so as not to give the impression you're going there to be seen, but to worship God. And your Father, who sees the inner life, will respond to you.

Or take another, more famous passage, a few lines later. In King James, Matthew 6:28-34 reads:

> And why take ye thought for raiment? Consider the lilies of the field, how they grow; they toil not, neither do they spin;
>
> And yet I say unto you, That even Solomon in all his glory was not arrayed like one of these.
>
> Wherefore, if God so clothe the grass of the field, which to day is, and to morrow is cast into the oven, shall he not much more clothe you, O ye of little faith?
>
> Therefore take no thought, saying, What shall we eat? Or, What shall we drink? Or, Wherewithal shall we be clothed?
>
> (For after all these things do the Gentiles seek): for your heavenly Father knoweth that ye have need of all these things.
>
> But seek ye first the kingdom of God, and his righteousness; and all these things shall be added unto you.
>
> Take therefore no thought for the morrow: for the morrow shall take thought for the things of itself. Sufficient unto the day is the evil thereof.

Jordan renders this advice as:

> And what's all this big to-do over clothing? Look yonder at that field of flowers, how they're growing. They do no housework and no sewing. But I'm telling you, not even Solomon in all his finery was ever dressed up like one of them. Well then, if God so clothes the flowers of the field, which are blooming today and are used for kindling tomorrow, won't he do even more for you, you spiritual runts? So cut out your anxious talk about 'what are we gonna eat, and what are we gonna drink, and what are we gonna wear.' For the people of the

world go tearing around after all these things. Listen, your spiritual father is quite aware that you've got to have all such stuff. Then set your heart on the God Movement and its kind of life, and all these things will come as a matter of course. Don't worry over the future; let the future worry over itself. Each day has enough troubles of its own.

Jordan's translations, in one sense, are ordinary, for he did no more than what preachers do every day – turn murky Bible verses into plain English. But Jordan went further; he hoped to eliminate misinterpretations, for like Jesus, he too had suffered at the hands of fellow churchmen. The Cotton Patch New Testament put Jesus' life directly into worshippers' hands, asked readers to grapple with Jesus' ideas rather than the preacher's gloss on them; made Jesus human, familiar, not an object of fear or pity or adulation.

The translations were consistent with the spirit behind Koinonia and the Fund for Humanity, and ultimately Habitat for Humanity, because they stressed the need to treat others' ills as one's own, to walk the Christian talk. *Fellowship*: Jordan's multifarious endeavors all led to that one goal, and it's both striking and disheartening to realize that his Bible translations 'unfellowed' him in some clerical minds.

Jordan's New Testament remains in print and continues to sell in respectable numbers. (My copy of *The Cotton Patch Version of Matthew and John* – subtitled 'A modern translation with a Southern accent, fervent, earthy, rich in humor' – is from the 24th printing.) But more people have encountered the work on stage or through television, for Jordan's testament was turned into a musical called "Cotton Patch Gospel" in 1981. (Below right, a poster put out by the musical's publisher and licensor.) Though late to the party – "Jesus Christ Superstar" and "Godspell" and "Joseph and the Amazing Technicolor Dreamcoat" popularized the 'Jesus genre' a decade earlier – it's often performed at churches, Christian schools and colleges, and the occasional professional theater. With music and lyrics by singer/activist Harry Chapin – who claimed to be 'born' to write the

show, and who finished the work a few months before his fatal car accident – the musical was called "a joyous triumph" by *The New York Times*. *Rolling Stone* said "The Cotton Patch Gospel" contained some of Chapin's best work.

The show – judging from the commercial video release of a 1980's Atlanta production – is true to both the humor and tragedy of Jordan's Bible story. The Southern vernacular sets an easy, aw-shucks tone, and Jesus (played by Tom Key, below, in a 2004 showing of his "Revelations Project," and who not only conceived the "Cotton Patch" adaptation but plays Matthew, Peter, Herod, Satan, Judas, and Pilate) is more perplexed than saintly – a former-day Hamlet, wanting to do the right thing but unsure of his courage and methods. Matthew narrates Jesus' story from "a simple, honest, and functional" set – one the early Christians designed and built themselves, according to the stage directions, because "they believe in what they have experienced." The link with Habitat is unmistakable, if unintentional.

Matthew walks on stage following a country-folk song about a possible "second coming" in Gainesville, Georgia, "a hell of a place to be heaven sent." He tells the story of Joe Davidson, a man who considered his fiancée Mary Hagler to be "a nice girl from a nice southern family" until she became pregnant without his help...at which point Joe wonders "how he would get his football jacket back." But an angel tells Joe about the Holy Spirit, and the Second Coming, and Joe believes. The couple marries: as instructed, Joe names the child Jesus, to which "every aunt, cousin, and great-grandmother objects because no one had ever heard the name Jesus before."

Mary, traveling to Atlanta with Joe to face an income-tax audit, gives birth to Jesus in an abandoned trailer behind the Dixie-Delite Motor Lodge.

Three scholars arrive, drawn by a bright star they followed from the Orient. Believing the baby will one day become Georgia's governor, the men present Jesus with "a gold American Express Card, some candles that put off a smell like fresh peaches, and a large, expensive-looking bottle of Jade East." Herod, it seems, has heard the same future-governor prophecy – probably from the National Enquirer, for that's how the governor (Matthew says) learned of the virgin birth. Herod orders the newborn killed, but the Davidsons, forewarned, have already fled.

Joe and Mary eventually realize that Jesus is not like other kids, since he constantly quotes the Testament and his lemonade stand never runs dry. (Mary remembers "all the things that Jesus said and did and wrote them down faithfully in her baby book.") Jesus grows even more Bible-conscious in adulthood, not looking for trouble but finding it by saying provocative things like "Man doesn't live by grits alone" and, during his own I.R.S. audit, that he neither had income, nor needed it. "People are real generous to us," Jesus tells Matthew, his tax auditor. "I tell them about my Father and make them well, and they do nice things for my followers and me. We have a wonderful time." Matthew, convinced of Jesus' power and sincerity, becomes a follower himself.

The musical tracks Jesus' life fairly closely, though with an emphasis on the power of the media, the corruptions of wealth, and the institutional allegiances of the organized church. Jesus brings a senator's daughter back from the dead; is frustrated that newspapers play up his miracles, not his philosophy or message; stands by helplessly as Las Vegas-based television preachers sing about having a "blind date with God," run ocean-liner pilgrimages "to the Holy Land and Hong Kong," or say Jesus must be in league with Satan because he cures people for free. Jesus walks on water (Peter, here called 'Rock,' says "that's the biggest duck I ever seen in my life!"), struggles with being a polarizing celebrity, and feeds five thousand people with "five boxes of Nabiscos, two cans of sardines."

Jesus' doings brand him a troublemaker, and he's arrested after failing to curtail his challenge, implicit and explicit, to civic, religious, and economic authorities. Some followers want him to lead a revolution, but Jesus refuses to become a powerful, all-providing celebrity who plays favorites and indulges in luxury. "[A]nybody who puts his possessions above me is not my man," Jesus says, "and anybody who will not accept his own lynching and share my life is not my man." And he is lynched, of course, after Pilate decides to send Jesus into exile, knowing martyrdom would only increase Jesus' power. The lynch mob is led by the KKK.

On the following Sunday, Matthew says, Jesus

> nearly gave everyone at the Big R Barbecue cardiac arrest when he walked through, and I mean *through*, the door. But then he ordered a cup of coffee and a pecan pie, ate it right in front of them, and that really put away their doubts.

Jesus, still more man than divinity, then stands on a table and gushes "It worked! It worked! I'm here."

The "Cotton Patch" musical broke no records in New York – 193 off-off-Broadway performances – but it's said to be the longest-running play in Dallas and Atlanta. And it still raises hackles, for this Jesus not only doubts and angers but tells jokes and weeps in fear. Many Christians were upset by a wise-cracking, deep-feeling Jesus, Jordan believed, because he seemed like a regular guy, an average Joe, the boy next door – and implied that the ability to act like Jesus, to walk the talk, lay within everyone...which was, of course, the point.

Tom Key, in a recent re-issue of Jordan's *The Cotton Patch Version of Matthew and John*, notes that opponents have taken out full-page newspaper advertisements to call his musical "blasphemy," that productions have been shut down following charges of sacrilege. (After one Kentucky run in 1999 the producer was handed a note reading, "I will pray for your mortal soul as you burn in hell.") Key also notes that his publicist brought out the vital distinction between the "Cotton Patch Gospel" and both "Jesus Christ Superstar" and "Godspell" when she said the latter were "about a man who became a God, but Cotton Patch Gospel is about a God who became a man."

Heroism, in both Jordan's and Habitat's world, is coming to understand that faith is a two-way street – that God has faith in man, too. And when Jordan's all-too-human Jesus puts a mirror up to members of the audience, they often squirm at the reflection.

The Cotton Patch New Testament was not, of course, the only arrow in Jordan's philosophical quiver. But it was the most effective, because the translation soft-pedaled Jordan's socio-political-religious beliefs: embedded in Jesus' story, they seemed more like truisms than a Georgia preacher's personal argument. Jordan's earlier social analyses are worth revisiting, however, not only for their wit and intelligence, but because they highlight the contradiction between words and work, form and substance, faith and action (you could well add *mind and body*). Jordan's inability to resolve this dualism at Koinonia Farm may have resulted from his abiding faith in reason (perhaps a contradiction in terms, but perhaps not): Fuller's ability, at Habitat, to transcend that dualism can be attributed to his salesman's optimism, his refusal to be flummoxed, angered, or sidetracked by inconsistency.

Jordan, by contrast, couldn't let sleeping dogs lie, especially when the dog was the Christian church. Following the desegregation cases of the 1950's, for instance, he said

> it burns my heart out that the Supreme Court is making pagans be more Christian than the Bible is making Christians be Christians.... The sit-ins never would have been necessary if Christians had been sitting down together in church at Christ's table these many years.

He didn't need to add that whites and blacks were breaking bread together at Koinonia since the 1940's.

The church, moreover, regularly overlooked the New Testament's very clear message concerning money. Loving money is called the "root of all evil" in Paul's first epistle to Timothy; and Jesus said a camel can pass more easily through the eye of a needle "than for a rich man to enter the kingdom of God," and in Jerusalem, threw the merchants and money-changers out of the temple. In the Cotton Patch version of this last scene, those with money are presumed to be "church people," so Jesus, in Jordan's view,

> pitched out the whole finance committee, tore up the investment and endowment records, and scrapped the long-range expansion plans. 'My house shall be known for its commitment to God,' he shouted, 'but you have turned it into a religious racket!'

In Jordan's view the church, too quick to take its cues from the wider culture, failed to understand the distinction between value and price, spiritual worth and physical assets. Rather than pointing out the reductive nature of market economies – which prize decorative gold and rubies far more than roofs without leaks, shoes without holes – the church participated in this mis-measurement. Mistaking means for ends, it built up treasures of its own, and became like that rich man – the model rejected by Fuller the Millionaire – shocked at finding he couldn't buy his way past the Pearly Gates.

Jesus was "a penniless tramp," Jordan wrote, "a high-minded hobo" who told his disciples to "follow me" and thus incarnate the Word (which was, in Jordan's view, mere prologue to Action). But only exceptional priests and pastors truly followed Jesus, allowed themselves to believe that spreading the word was the first step in a Christ-inspired cultural revolution. Jordan's Jesus believed "what you value and what you really are is one and the same," that Christians should hold the spiritual dearer than the material. Wealth, at bottom, was "worm food," gone with the wind, so why spend your life "striving for something that was nothing"? Wasn't that idea in every New Testament, no matter the language?

Jordan's rant – and his sermons could be rants, bitter and excessive – didn't end there. The New Testament says explicitly that men "cannot serve God and Mammon," but Jordan's Jesus goes on to warn "I don't want you to be money addicts" (the concept that pinioned Fuller). Furthermore, Jordan argued, Jesus didn't say you *shouldn't* serve two masters, but that you *can't*: the road simply forked, so following Mammon meant, necessarily, rejecting honest-to-God Christianity. (Above right, a 19th-century French rendition of Mammon.) Jesus tells a number of parables – "comparisons," in Jordan's world – along this line, and one involves the rich farmer who thinks, after putting a vast harvest in storage, "soul, you got it made. Recline, dine, wine, and shine." God, however, tells the farmer, "You nitwit. This very night, they are demanding your soul of you" – 'they' being his fields, his barns, his hoarded food. In Jordan's words, "This guy didn't die. Something more tragic than that happened to him. He lived. He lived in bondage to the very things he thought would serve him."

Following Mammon, Jordan wrote, is "easier than falling off a log." And both the state and the church encouraged that fall, believing economic enrichment carried no downside. The church wanted huge buildings and bejeweled crosses; the state, giant trade surpluses and expanding economies. In one series of sketches – which Jordan called his "goofed-up Bible" – Mammon tells a man going deeper into debt to buy a new car, "This night, thou hast become a great American. All thy debts will greatly stimulate the economy. And wilt not thy slavery enrich others? So is he that accumulates many debts and is faithful to Mammon."

Dallas Lee is close to the mark when he writes that Jordan and Fuller, while organizing the Fund for Humanity in 1968, had decided to "wage a war on wealth." Money was largely responsible for man's "estrangement from God," Jordan believed, and from other people as well (as Fuller knew from personal experience). And the Bible told Jordan, again and again, he was on the right track – the New Testament saying "if a guy takes your shirt, don't stop him from taking your undershirt" (Cotton Patch Luke, 6:27), and the Old Testament, that all property is God's. People were no more than custodians of the Lord's riches, and those who claimed otherwise were men of Mammon.

And what should you do with God's property? Make it fruitful – and not only for yourself. If given talents, you multiplied them; if seeds, you planted. But could you rent your land to another? To make a little ready cash to buy, say, a new television, a new lawn-mower? No – because that meant profiting from the other fellow's sweat, not your own, meant serving Mammon by way of God's possessions. Jordan saw such misplaced service all around him in the 1960's: hundreds of Georgia farmers, white and black alike, losing their land to absentee owners (most of them commercial banks and, coincidentally, Connecticut-based insurance companies). Jordan devoted a 1968 lecture to this peculiar state of affairs, demonstrating throughout his ability to marshal arcane details in support of a larger theme.

In the 1930's, he noted, about 15,000 people, 10,000 of them black, lived in Sumter County, where Koinonia was located. By 1960, the population had dropped to 5,000, of whom 3,000 were black. Where did those other 7,000 blacks go? Thousands went to Hartford, Connecticut, which by 1968 had a larger black population than Sumter County, making Hartford "the sister city of Americus." Sumter's emigrants had simply followed the money – their own money, Jordan argued, because the insurance industry, long centered in Hartford, held billions of dollars in farm mortgages.

Every year Koinonia itself sent $2,000 in mortgage interest to Hartford – "annual tribute," Jordan called it – and many neighbors did the same...though perhaps writing 'Boston' on the envelope. Boston's John Hancock insurance company "owns about half of Sumter County," Jordan said. "Got mortgages on it. And they let it out for a little word called interest. They are very interested in Sumter County." And so was Prudential Insurance, Jordan continued, because "Prudential *understands*, I mean it understands, how to keep people poor."

Jordan gives a quick lesson in economics. In 1930 you could buy a farm in Sumter County for, on average, $3,290. You might have to take on some debt, but it was still possible, then, for John Q. Public to save enough money to purchase property outright, free and clear. By 1960, however, the average farm was valued at $61,218; by 1968, the price had rocketed to $137,000. Debt was now unavoidable – and so was the need to keep up with the Joneses, and not just socially, either. If Farmer Jones bought a shiny new baler or harvester, at so many dollars a month, that made his farm more efficient and more productive, well, Farmer Smith felt he had to do the same...and the insurance company was glad to make the loan. As Jordan would say on other occasions, "Most money is taken not with a pistol but with a pencil."

Jordan illustrates the problem with the rock-and-a-hard-place troubles of Rob Hamilton, his Koinonia neighbor. When automation came to Sumter, Jordan says, Hamilton bought big tractors, big combines, to stay abreast of his fellow farmers, with John Hancock providing the capital. And those machines did help Hamilton farm more efficiently...but drove his profits *down*.

With a farm-machinery debt of $120,000, Hamilton paid the bank $9,600 in interest every year – an unremarkable figure until you examine the accounting ledger. If Hamilton planted his 300 acres in corn – which he couldn't, at least 50 acres were marginal farmland – his harvest would be, on average, 40 bushels of corn per acre, or 12,000 bushels. Corn futures, when Jordan told this story, sold for about a dollar per bushel, so Hamilton would gross $12,000, or net $3,600 after expenses (the average profit on a bushel of corn in 1968 was 30 cents). The result? After months of unrelenting work, the constant pressure of uncertain weather and unpredictable trade, Hamilton's debt to Hancock grew by another $6,000.

Farmer Hamilton read the writing on the wall. "Rob is going into bankruptcy," Jordan said. "He's selling his farm and he's moving to town and the Negro who is living with him will be moving to Hartford."

Jordan couldn't prevent the men from leaving. But through the brand-new Fund for Humanity he did buy, for $80,000, Hamilton's 300 acres. The land was already spoken for: two farmers, one black and one white, would work the farm in partnership. "We're saying to them," Jordan went on,

> This is your inheritance. Neither of you could inherit it from your earthly father, but you are inheriting it from your spiritual father. The land is the Lord's and, as in all inheritances, you do not pay interest. You do not pay principal on it. This is yours. So we're substituting a word that we call 'usership' for 'ownership.' It's not yours to own, but it's yours to use for as long as you want to use it. When you make 12,000 bushels of corn, you don't have to pay Hancock or Prudential anything. You make it by the sweat of your brow....

The catch? "[Y]ou should be willing to share; and, out of grace and gratitude, you should be willing to give something to the Fund for Humanity."

Jordan, in brief, turned textbook economics on its head – encouraged people to work for gratitude instead of cash, for the well-being of the community rather than individual financial reward. He would retain the incentives of capitalism but change the payoff...and without enlisting the government, for he knew institutions could be just as self-serving as people, and less accountable. The key was convincing the average Jane and Joe that giving – just as Jesus said – was more important, and more satisfying, than getting. The Fund for Humanity, he said,

> is not like a government handout. You give nobody nothing: you just take the foot off his neck. You're not training him in dependency like many government programs do.... It isn't helping people even to help themselves. It's helping people to help others...and I think it's going to give a motivation...that just making money by itself does not have.

At the Fund for Humanity's formation a few months earlier, Jordan said it should begin – begin! – by purchasing a million acres of land. "At $300 an acre," he reasoned, "that's only $300 million – that's only five days of the Vietnamese war." The Fund never grew that large, of course, but it's a good bet Jordan would accept a million people housed, in homes built by unpaid volunteers and sold without interest, as a reasonable substitute.

Six

Amateur Hour

I can't identify the exact moment when I admitted to suffering from 'Habititis.' For years I said I was "doing research"; was working on a book about Habitat, trying to understand the organization from the inside out. I'd read everything about Habitat I could lay my hands on; grilled volunteers over lunch; attended affordable-housing conferences; worked on a score of build sites, including one in Harlem during Habitat's annual Jimmy Carter Work Project; toured Carter's birthplace outside Plains, Georgia, and Habitat headquarters in Americus, where I also interviewed Fuller; traveled to Guatemala with one of Habitat's "Global Village" home-building teams; written articles about Habitat for local publications; volunteered to run Housatonic Habitat's website and newsletter; taken hundreds and hundreds of pages of notes, lay awake nights trying to figure out how the Habitat pieces fit together. I was a journalist still, or so I thought, trying to get "the Habitat story" down in black and white.

But I forever crossed the line, I see in retrospect, when I organized a 'Tropical Build' for Housatonic Habitat with its sister affiliate in the Dominican Republic. I'd sworn, after my first 'Global Village' build with Habitat, that I'd never go on another one, for that week in Totonicapan, Guatemala, proved a "peak" life experience...and I assumed any similar trip would disappoint. (On the following page, a Guatemalan girl studying in her Habitat home.) Within a few

months, however, I was anxious to build again in another country, any country, to feel again that I was filling an honest-to-God need – an actual want, not some manufactured "want" invented on Madison Avenue, Wall Street, Silicon Valley. And if I *created* an international trip, I could give my privileged fellow *norteamericanos* the chance to live the Habitat ethos for an entire week, to "get it" on a fundamental level. If every U.S. citizen worked hard on somebody else's truly significant problem, saw what progress could be made through a few hundred hours of collective sweat...well, who knows what might happen.

I'd caught the "bug" in spades, and Housatonic Habitat's "Tropical Build" is now an annual event.

Altarita's specialty was straightening nails. She'd find a container – a coffee can was good, but a ball cap would do, or a t-shirt pulled up and into a cradle – and walk the jobsite in her bare feet. She'd end up with a dozen or more nails, some rusted but most shiny, since – with each volunteer having donated $450 to the cause – we *norteamericanos* had raised plenty of money for new building materials. But like most people in the Dominican Republic, Altarita was used to scrounging: her own house, a few feet away, was assembled (you can't really say "built") from palm fronds, plastic tarps, planking salvaged from wrecked boats. It was a hovel, in truth, which fourteen-year-old Altarita shared with her mother and an indeterminate number of siblings and relatives.

Altarita would place a nail – J-shaped, an L if it had bounced off a knot – on a scrap of plywood, bent side up. She tapped the bump lightly at first, getting a rhythm, then harder, her hand halfway up the hammer's handle. Her grip was technically wrong, but it worked: in thirty seconds the nail was straight. No doubt she could work faster, create her own little production line...but why? No reason to hurry

here in Paraiso, to become efficient, because labor was dirt cheap; the warehouse and offices of the local coffee co-op were destroyed by Hurricane Georges in 1998, and the re-building, three years later, had yet to begin. (At right, a Paraiso Habitat official – Lorenzo, one of my favorite people in the whole world – shows off a house built in the hurricane's wake.) Altarita, in any case, was herself a volunteer. Her family was too poor to afford even the minimal payments – perhaps $50 a month – required of Habitat homeowners in this small fishing village twenty miles from Haiti (which shares with the DR the island of Hispaniola, where Christopher Columbus was originally buried).

It's the children that make you want to go native, à la Gauguin. Walking to the day's worksite, you'll often feel a tug on your hand, and look down to see that a child – perhaps a three-year-old, a five-year-old – has placed a small hand in your own. He may laugh at your surprise, or she may not even bother to look up: in either case, you know you're trusted, no questions asked. Habitat has come to town, and we volunteers seem to represent something wondrous – half fairy godmother, half circus clown. We entertain the kids just by speaking bad Spanish and trying to do good things.

We're more serious on site. The houses resemble those built by Fuller in Zaire before founding Habitat – concrete block, less than 500 square feet, minimal plumbing, just enough windows to light the place. The roofs are very different, however, for the Caribbean has hurricanes: rather than putting up tin, or tile, or fiberglass, we pour roofs in the Dominican Republic, up to 15 tons of concrete per house. The pour must be done all at once, and within a few hours, so the slab won't crack and leak, and is solid enough to withstand 100-mile-per-hour winds. And rushing, debris-laden water, too: if the gales don't flatten the house, the accompanying flash floods might.

You always remember your first poured-concrete roof. (The photo on the next page shows the earlier stages of a pour.) Mine was on a site not far from "downtown" Paraiso, a ten-minute, uphill walk from the

hotel (put up to house the doctors and do-gooders who set up the village's health clinic). Sandy, the local site manager, was a little scary: he always wore dark glasses, spoke little, regularly showed exasperation, and – unusually for a Dominican – rarely smiled. The family we were building with, on the other hand, welcomed us as long-lost kin: its patriarch, Bienvenito, proposed to one of our crewmates, Maredith, within hours (she spoke some Spanish, and while greatly flattered, declined). We soon learned that in Paraiso practically the entire population claims to be "primos," or first cousins – blood relations, almost without exception. (The same is still true in parts of the American South, as Jimmy Carter notes in his book *Turning Point*, tactfully writing that it is "sometimes difficult for non-Southerners to understand how stable the population of rural Southern communities had been" since the European settlement. His future wife Rosalynn, for example, was "one of the few female residents in Plains who was not related to me, at least within the last 120 years or so.")

Sandy and his assistants were already lugging bags of cement when we arrived at the build site around 8. They'd already installed wooden headers over the windows and doors: it was time to start mixing cement. A couple days earlier we'd used a portable, diesel-powered cement-mixer at another site, but the crew gave up after the drive chain dropped off every fifteen minutes – it was faster to mix the cement by hand. So that's what we did at the upper site, a job guaranteed to give you a backache and blisters. For the latter I'd learned my lesson in Guatemala: I duct-taped my fingers.

Pedrito led the cement carriers. We were used to seeing him in the forefront; he was Haitian, his skin black as an oil slick, and when he wasn't working like a dog he was joking around or singing or rolling his eyes. Haitians, in theory, are hated by Dominicans because they often slip illegally over the border and work for less than the natives, not unlike Mexicans in the U.S.: moreover, Haitians generally speak French, not Spanish, and are descended from Africans rather than Europeans and Indians. (The Indian blood that flows through native

Dominican veins is not local, however, because the Spanish, after wiping out Hispaniola's original human population, brought over Indian slaves from South America.) Pedrito had long been accepted by the community, however...though on site, at least, he was still called "Africa."

We fell into the line, carrying the cement bags – 94 pounds each – from the street to the jobsite, where Pedrito and other workers were making a large circle of sand. So went traditional concrete-making

in the DR: forming a six-foot 'volcano' out of sand, covering it with cement powder, pouring water into the crater, and slowly pushing sections of the volcano into the middle for mixing. (Left, a mortar volcano before the water goes on.) It seems ingenious to the novice eye: you could make any size batch of concrete you wanted, depending on how much volcano-wall you pushed in, and could easily adjust the mixture by shoveling in more water, more cement, more sand (or gravel, if you were making an aggregate concrete rather than mortar).

I was familiar with the volcano technique from other Global Village trips, but Pedrito's volcano was huge, perhaps 15 feet across. He'd be mixing half the roof concrete all at once, knowing the job had to be done quickly...and that he'd have lots of help. If there was one thing we *norteamericanos* could do without getting in the way too much, it was mixing cement.

Four or five of us could work the volcano at once, Pedrito occasionally adding water from a hose as the mixture became clay-like, too dry. From time to time he'd jump in and do some mixing himself, turning over spadefuls three times faster than we did, and without apparent effort. I wondered, at first, whether he was trying to show us the best way to mix cement, or was hoping to hurry us along, but concluded that not working made him nervous. He was paid to sweat, not supervise; managing this mostly white-skinned crew, grabbing the hose and watering where necessary, hardly counted. I wondered, too, what he thought of us. *Is life so easy in the States they must come here to know hard work? So dull, they'd mix cement on vacation?*

Seeing the Caribbean from the rooftop, watching high-sea freighters through palm fronds, was invigorating at first, but the work was wearing, to the point of exhaustion. (Right, the locals do much of the muscle-intensive work.) Three, four hours in the sun; transporting 200-odd buckets of *mescla* (mixture); mixing and shoveling, mixing and shoveling, as if you were on a chain gang – you understood the impetus for labor-saving devices, the unsung skills involved in physical work. We lived for breaks…and the future homeowner, luckily, had limes and mangos and cocoa pods hanging from her trees. She made *batidas*, the local fruit drink, in an electric blender in a make-shift, outdoor kitchen, and handed them out with a broad smile. Watching her cleave fruit with a machete, you understood – if simultaneously ignoring the nearby hovels, the construction debris, the knowledge that suffering was only a storm away – the inspiration for Club Med. *Take the best, discard the rest*: copy the trappings of a culture, sanitize its spirit.

A native crew, as we mixed concrete, built a plywood platform against the front of the house. Two men shoveled *mescla* onto the platform: two others clambered onto it (the plywood had been recycled so many times, we wondered if the platform would hold) and re-shoveled the cement into wheelbarrows on the roof. A teenager – an apprentice, no doubt – rolled the wheelbarrow along planks to the far corner of the roof, and dumped it, moving the planks every few minutes. In less than two hours, the temporary roof – held up by a trusswork of plywood panels and 2x4 "deadmen" – held six inches of concrete, reinforced with a rebar grid. The technique is known the world over…which is why you may hear, when a busload of dirty, sunburned gringos passes a construction site in Latin America, "Hey, guys, let's go ahead and finish it!"

But we *norteamericanos* don't do any platform shoveling, not today, we don't have the stamina or skill. (But it is done: Vin Masotta, on the left in the picture to the right, takes a turn in 2004, and later dead-

pans, "I thought I was either going to end up a local hero, or dead.") There's poetry in it: perfectly timed movements, so shovels don't clash, so spade-loads hit the wheelbarrow in sequence, so the pace is predictable, unchanging. Little rhythm means little work: if we volunteers shoveled here, now, we'd be more hindrance than help. I understood, then, that our physical presence is a liability. Habitat volunteers provide the capital, get the ball rolling, ensure that effort is expended, that deadlines are met…but in person, we're mostly in the way. And that's okay, because house-building, at bottom, is almost beside the point, the icing on the cake. What we're really building is relationships, a new framework through which to see the world. *What's so great about being Number One, the lone super-power, if you've forgotten how to care?*

We're taught unwittingly, in spite of ourselves, in spite of experience. Reading picture books to the children we find the kids don't fight. (Below, the kids gather at the Hotel Paraiso before dinnertime, knowing they'll get to play checkers or dominoes, and maybe get some leftovers, too.) And we discover, if a volunteer's book or backpack or bottle is accidentally left on site, it magically turns up at the hotel.

But give a book to a child, and the book will make the rounds, in a different hovel every night, transformed into community property. It's an idea Habitat has accepted on the structural level: even the poorest affiliates tithe 10 percent of their income to other affiliates, because the line between 'taker' and 'giver' is fluid, because everybody has something to share.

It dawned on me, watching Altarita straighten nails, that Habitat put you outside quotidian experience – allowed you to be your best self, a child again, ignorant and impressionable and open-minded. You absorbed rather than judged, listened rather than held forth; you learned what you couldn't learn, refused to learn, in your workaday life. The samba from Wendy, who emerged from her hovel every day (shared with her mother and five siblings) to study law in the provincial capital (that's Wendy, on the far right, with her sister Pilar, dressed up for the Dominican Independence Day *carnaval*); beach-baseball from 12-year-old Dolio, a Denzel Washington look-alike who grabbed a palm-frond shaft, filled your hands with stones, and motioned for you to pitch (no wonder the Dominican Republic produces more major-league baseball players per capita than any other country); Francesca, legs crippled into an 'O', but who kept up with the other kids without complaint, and was treated, in turn, like any other child.

And Altarita, straightening nails, helping to build the home in which Wendy, the village's golden girl, would soon live. I watched through five nails, six, seven, until she handed me the hammer, handle first. I arranged a disfigured nail on a plywood scrap, and after a few mistakes, a few glancing blows, I, too, had a straight-ish nail. A half-smile played across Altarita's face – not the incandescent grin we saw from time to time, blindingly white teeth against deep-dark skin, but a thoughtful smile, one of knowledge. She was proud, and surprised, to be teaching a norteamericano something, and yes, she taught more than nail-straightening. *To hell with the experts, the professionals, the do-it-this-wayers; the pendulum has swung, it's time for the amateurs again.*

Seven

"Everyone Together"

Koinonia did not fall apart after Jordan's death. It would have without Fuller: the farm's re-invention as Koinonia Partners provided a broader base, a higher level of energy, put the community ahead of the curve once more. New volunteers came, for longer periods, to work in the partnership industries, which now included sewing clothes and throwing pots as well as processing pecans. Change had been a constant before Fuller's arrival – unavoidably, given Koinonia's dedication to tolerance and consensus – but he demonstrated that change could be managed...and was essential to the partnership's survival. In 1951, a full member of Koinonia was required to sign a document giving all possessions to the farm for use by the entire group; in 1969, a year after the Fullers moved in, members could loan their assets to the community and draw a salary. As one scholar has noted, if Koinonia Farm stressed communal living, Koinonia Partners focused on individual work within a communal context.

And the work that captured many imaginations, to an extent no one had foreseen, was home building. Snapping lines, laying block, nailing shingles, hanging doors; there was something new every day, some novel obstacle to overcome, and you never knew, going in, whether you'd be teacher or student, expert or apprentice, brains or muscle. And the experience brought home more than the idea of building community; it embodied the thought, for both volunteer home-builders and future homeowners. Everyone sweated together, marveled at the like-mindedness of such different personalities and perspectives, and felt themselves part of Something Big...and soon to grow much bigger.

Jordan's shoes were difficult to fill, but Fuller slipped them on with characteristic optimism. He put up new buildings to expand pecan processing, and the mail-order business increased by half. He encouraged various new partnership ventures such as corn production and cattle ranching. Linda Fuller helped organize a sewing shop for local women, set up a day-care program called the Koinonia Child Development Center. And Fuller made sure these endeavors were publicized, especially the one that struck the strongest chord – home-building. With Jordan gone, he oversaw the completion of Koinonia Village – two dozen homes on 100-by-200-foot lots, and the planning of another development, Forest Park, of 32 homes on three-quarter-acre lots.

As with Tougaloo College, though, the fit between Fuller and Koinonia was imperfect. Jordan was a Jeffersonian philosopher-farmer, loved the solitude of his writing shack (despite saying Koinonia declined large monetary gifts because they would cause partners to "quit growing peanuts and start discussing theology"). Fuller wasn't like that: he was a man of deeds, of movement, and still, being in his mid-30's, very ambitious. When asked to run something, he expected to run it as he saw fit, and with dispatch. While Jordan could thunder in Jesus' name, could justify his own autocratic streak in moral and theological terms, Fuller had no convenient rationalization for his take-charge personality, his failure, often, to seek out others' opinions. He loved the idea of putting faith into action, but wanted to do so *right now*; he didn't like waiting for details, feeling like a bully or nag, while doing the Lord's work.

Three years after Jordan's death, Fuller resigned his Koinonia directorship and picked up his Bible. He spent a month in Jordan's writing shack, reading and studying and thinking. *How can I be God's servant and a project's master simultaneously? Listen without judging, contribute without leading, disagree without hurting?* He expected, after those weeks of reflection, to step back into Koinonia as one Christian servant among many, but discovered the farm had selected new leaders: that his opinions and experience no longer held sway, that he was just one of the multitude once again.

It was a major comedown, however necessary for the partnership – painful for Fuller personally, and wasteful of his skills. *The Fund for Humanity is a wonderful thing, Fuller told himself, but it's a baby step when giant strides are needed,* required! *I can't hide this light anymore: my vision no longer fits the Koinonia mold.* Fuller still believed in partnership, in service, in duty…but would realize them more effectively, more efficiently, more lastingly, in another inflection. Yes, he could continue to do God's work at Koinonia, but could do it better elsewhere – and his way, as well as His way.

The Fullers left Americus for a brief vacation, hoping a trip to Florida would once again inspire a project that took full advantage of their interests and dedication. And it did, for Fuller found himself thinking back to Mbandaka, the remote Congolese city, 400 miles from Kinshasa, they'd visited on the U.C.C. mission six years earlier, in 1966. (Fund for Humanity homes being built in Zaire, above, in 1976.) Fuller had met Disciples of Christ missionaries there, heard them talk about developing a block-and-sand business to build not only homes for the urban poor but a skilled, self-sufficient, hopeful community. *We've done partnership housing at Koinonia, Fuller thought: Couldn't we do it in Africa, too? Where the need is even greater, where a block-making business already exists?*

From a Tallahassee hotel room Fuller phoned the church official who had organized the couple's first trip to the Congo. Fuller asked after the Mbandaka block project, about church sponsorship, about volunteer opportunities. "Millard," the man replied, "your call is providential. If you had called two days ago I would have said 'No,' but only yesterday a representative of the Zaire church was in my office asking for someone to help with development. I told them we didn't have anyone – but now I can tell them we do!"

The Fullers returned to Africa in July, 1973.

Fuller began working with concrete blocks at the age of ten, on a farm owned by his father. The elder Fuller, a grocer in the cotton-mill town of Lanett, Alabama, had bought the 400-acre property for $1500 in 1945 – a bargain, then, for marginal farmland. It was called 'two-nigger farm' by local whites, being worked by a pair of black families living in rundown shacks.

Fuller's father, the son of a sharecropper himself, was known as a decent man, and perhaps that's why the tenants – for whom speaking up, in many areas of the South, was still dangerous – were willing to voice their frustrations about the hardscrabble farm. They complained that German prisoners of war, on lumber-cutting work-crews from a nearby internment camp, had been eating their corn, raw; but that issue was now moot, for the work crews had left. (In Zaire thirty years later, Fuller would run into a German who had served on a Lanett P.O.W. work-crew – run into him for the second time, perhaps, because young Fuller befriended the German prisoners just as young Jordan had black convicts in Georgia.) The tenants' other major problem was easier to address: the miserable condition of their homes.

One house was beyond repair, father Fuller decided, but the other could be saved. So he, Millard, and resident sharecropper Bud Lancaster set to work: shoring up the foundation with concrete blocks, replacing the swiss-cheese roof, adding siding to the outside walls because wind and rain blew right through the original planking. For the ceilings -- the shack had none, before – the Fullers used packing cases from coffins, and then painted the interior walls (after Bud consulted with his wife) bright pink. "Bud and Mattie were ecstatic," Fuller would write of the Lancasters. "And I discovered, to my delight, that their joy was also a personal thrill to me."

The houses Fuller put up in Mbandaka – a town established by journalist-cum-explorer Henry Morton Stanley (shown in pith helmet at right) – weren't so different. The initial plan called for 100 cement-block, tin-roofed homes built in a single neighborhood; they would have detached community kitchens, following local custom, but neither plumbing nor electricity.

The regional government of Zaire (map at right, showing Mbandaka in the northwest) appreciated the help, for Mbandaka's population had grown from 30,000 to 150,000 since the nation's independence thirteen years earlier, and thousands of new residents – most unemployed – were living in nothing but cardboard shantytowns.

Fuller had some quick talking to do nonetheless, especially after admitting that the project's sponsor, the Zairois Church of Christ, had promised no funding. Koinonia Partners had pledged $3,000, but Fuller didn't volunteer that information, preferring to say he was "building on faith" – and successfully, too, for he had already resurrected the nearby block-and-sand project. Inoperative when Fuller arrived ten weeks earlier, by the time of his housing pitch it was producing as many as 7500 blocks a month.

Days later the government handed over, gratis, a 35-acre property in the heart of Mbandaka. At Fuller's request, the mayor also loaned scores of workers to cut down palm trees and dig up the site's twenty-foot ant hills, for otherwise the three brand-new, never-been-used theodolites (surveying instruments, also on loan from the government, and whose name does *not* mean "seeing like God" in ancient Greek) would have been useless.

Fuller, when he first saw the land and its central location, was surprised to find it undeveloped. *Perhaps the land was too low, flooded during the rainy season?* But he soon realized the surrounding real estate, now built-up, was on equally low ground. And what about the property's funny name – 'Bokotola,' meaning 'Man who does not care for others'? A local priest answered his questions. The area was the city's color bar: Bokotola defined the edge of the white section of town, the line that blacks could cross to work but never to live.

Home contractors in the U.S. routinely complain about their difficulties – zoning regulations, uncooperative banks, change orders, infuriating clients, bad weather. But compared to Fuller's experience in Zaire, they have it easy. Theft, petty as well as grand, was rampant in Mbandaka, for President Joseph-Désiré Mobutu – who came to

power (shown on his throne, at right) after orchestrating, with U.S. support, the overthrow and execution of Patrice Lumumba, the country's first democratically elected leader – ran a kleptocracy. He later christened himself Mobutu Sese Seko Nkuku Wa Za Banga (one translation: "The all-powerful warrior who, because of his endurance and inflexible will to win, will go from conquest to conquest, leaving fire in his wake"), and was known as Mobutu Sese Seko for short.

Mobutu ruled to enrich himself, like his famous predecessor – King Leopold of Belgium (shown below), who owned the Congo personally between 1885 and 1908. Mobutu learned from the master: Leopold stripped the Congo of its rubber through slave labor, killing tens of millions of people in the process. In the 1890's one notorious Belgian official, Rene de Permentier, "had all the bushes and trees cut down around his house at Bokatola [sic] so that from his porch he could use passersby for target practice," writes Adam Hochschild in the Congolese history *King Leopold's Ghost*...and there's a good chance the Bokotola neighborhood was named after Permentier himself.

Tools regularly disappeared from the Bokotola worksite, equipment never arrived or was stranded at Customs for months, workers failed to show up due to illness or because Mobutu declared a sudden holiday; even basic commodities –oil, shovels – could be difficult, sometimes impossible to acquire. Bribery was routine, an accepted cost of doing business; the Fullers were arrested some two dozen times during their first few months in Zaire, on the presumption that all white people were rich and would quickly pay for their release. Fuller refused to go along, however, and it's easy to hear him explaining, in an ear-grating French drawl, that he had come to Zaire to help the police captain's mother, daughter, brother-in-law. The take-no-prisoners prisoner would eventually be released, unharmed and unrobbed.

But the project (shown nearly completed, below) came close to failure soon after the Fund for Humanity officially received the Bokotola land. Everything was in place: the survey was completed, the government had agreed to loan a bulldozer, an access road was being made, ground-breaking for the first house was less than a week away. Then a city official arrived, carrying a bill – for $50,000, the cost for 114 building permits. Fuller was stunned, said he'd fly back to America the next

day...and the fee fell 95%, to $2,300. So Fuller, predictably, went for broke, offering to pay only a token charge. The official agreed – but after 15 trips to the permit office over the next three weeks, Fuller remained empty-handed. He gave up: the Fund poured foundations, built walls, and ultimately held dedication ceremonies without being issued, or paying for, a single permit.

Fuller's stubbornness – you could say 'faith,' and Fuller would – was essential to the project's completion. Although Habitat, today, is careful not to impose American values on other cultures, in the 1970's Fuller constantly threatened and cajoled the locals, told supporters and government officials alike "I didn't come to Zaire to fritter away my time." And Fuller could justify such statements because his my-way remonstrances were coupled so closely to home building, to service; he derived personal satisfaction from the effort, certainly, but no economic benefit. Bokotola, he said time and again, was the workers' project; that the Zairois on site were building a community of their own, not a "little America," let alone a little Bethlehem. In the final analysis, he told workers, "a self-centered life is a self-destroying life" – a Christian view, but hardly exclusive to Christianity.

The message was powerful in a country more familiar with colonialism than self-determination, with dictatorship than democracy. As a Zairois colleague, the pastor Bolongwa, told Fuller, "You are the first person ever to talk to us in this way. In the past, men in this country worked out of two motivations: fear and absolute necessity. They were deathly afraid of the *mundele*" – the white man – "and they felt no interest in the company they worked for." From Fuller, he continued, the Zairois learned that things could change, that whites could be colleagues; that power could be shared, could do more than exploit.

When the Fullers returned to the U.S. in 1976, their three-year-old home-building mission embedded in the local culture, the neighborhood had a new name. It was re-christened 'Losanganya,' or 'Everyone together.'

Fuller, on his return to the U.S., looked up his old friends in Georgia. Koinonia was doing fairly well, the Forest Park development was nearly complete. Yes, the farm had survived…and so would Losanganya, also without him.

Did Fuller see the pattern? Once he set a project in motion, inspired a community, things began to snowball: the venture began to generate its own power. Fuller was unrivaled in his ability to come up with ideas, to produce a head of steam…but after that, he didn't need to be deeply involved. And in truth, because he had so much energy, because he liked being busy and in control, Fuller could become – much like Clarence Jordan – a pain in the neck. He'd challenge people, ask the impossible, make stalwarts feel they weren't doing enough; jump up on conference-room tables to make points, cause potential supporters to think him goofy; hug people who didn't want to be hugged, ally himself with people who proved unreliable. Linda (right, with Millard in 1974) put it this way, speaking for those charged with implementing her husband's over-the-top plans: "Millard has the visions, we get the nightmares."

Habitat's African origins are unknown to many supporters, who typically regard the organization as an exemplar of American know-how. But the African field-test was essential to Habitat's future accomplishments, because there Fuller saw, with his own eyes, the terrible consequences of colonialism, poverty, and racism...and recognized how joint home-building could bridge those cultural chasms. Clarence Jordan also noted the dangers of 'groupthink' – patriotism, he noted more than once, was "just another form of prejudice" – but his skill at argument tended to quash ideas different from his own. Fuller, by contrast, thrived on difference, on newness, on enthusiasm, and the African experience cemented his belief that energy and empowerment could build on one another, that faith and work went hand in hand.

What people needed, Fuller intuited, was a way to break free of old, destructive cultural identities without sacrificing their sense of self, their hard-won personal beliefs. But how? Fuller's answer: by offering people the chance to forge new identities – Christian identities, in Fuller's ideal – that brought a new set of powers, a new way of living, suggested growth rather than loss. And what produced a greater sense of power, of gain, than the ability to build a house, maybe an entire community, with your own hands? Fuller enjoyed such physical work himself, but his true calling was the stagecraft of Prospero (above right), making partners of people who were unskilled, uninvolved strangers five minutes before. A Prospero, that is, with a touch of Tom Sawyer (above left), for you need a lot of painters to raise and paint a fence stretching around the globe.

Fuller & Dees, Tougaloo, Koinonia, Mbandaka: Fuller's life before Habitat is a series of enthusiasms that eventually flagged. The decision to move on, in each case, seems easily explained – emotional crisis, malaise, frustration, homesickness – but the root cause lies deeper. Fuller wanted to stretch his talents to the limit, and that meant working on a large scale: only then would he have done his absolute best for God, have conquered his fundamental human selfishness by pushing his abilities to the limit. He wasn't going to be like that Atlanta pastor with the 'personnel problem' – ignoring the obvious, giving in to inertia, failing to right a long-standing wrong. He wasn't going to have to say on Judgment Day – as he imagined himself declaring after Linda left him eleven years earlier – "Lord, I sold a hell of a lot of cookbooks!"

In the fall of 1976 Fuller called another convention at Koinonia. Clarence Jordan loomed once more, though only in spirit, and would have appreciated that the meeting was driven more by practice than theory.

Fuller's vision called for a global organization that didn't get caught up in minutiae; that linked working social structures rather than "improved" them from a superficial outside perspective. The new organization, to be called Habitat for Humanity, would strive to bring out the best in people rather than point out their failings, would praise them for helping neighbors instead of condemning them for ancient prejudice. If Jordan represented opposition to the Old South, Fuller was a cheerleader for the New...and observant enough to realize that such tribalism played a major role in the world's problems.

The following year Fuller published, through an imprint of the YMCA (which had also printed books by Dale Carnegie, in 1920, as well as Clarence Jordan), a description of his African years. In the epilogue to *Bokotola* (original cover at right) he noted that Habitat for Humanity had just been formed "to raise funds, recruit personnel, and provide procedures and expertise for developing proper 'habitat' for God's people in need." He invited support from those "committed to serving in the name of Christ – Baptists, Methodists, Lutherans, Presbyterians, Quakers, Mennonites, Disciples, United Church of Christ people, Episcopalians, Catholics, and many others."

What's striking about the list, today, is its narrowness. Although Fuller always thought big, in 1976 he envisioned Habitat as a church-based project, a natural extension of the foreign-mission work central to the United Church of Christ in which Fuller grew up (and to Jordan's Southern Baptists, too). By the 1970's, however, such work was problematic, perceived both at home and abroad as colonialism with a clerical face. The days of Albert Schweitzer and Dr. Livingstone (supposedly "discovered" by Stanley, who claimed the Congo on King Leopold's behalf) were over: independence for undeveloped countries, thereafter, would be cultural as well as political. Christian mission work, which promoted church-going as well as education and health, was still practiced, but increasingly defined in native terms...which dovetailed well with the newborn Habitat's 'partnership' philosophy.

The fit was not coincidental. Fuller (below, at a Zairois Habitat ceremony in 1982) had learned the hard way that partnerships do not exist in name only; they must be worked at, cultivated, honored. As a lawyer, he knew the importance of gathering facts before passing judgment, and as a sales-savvy businessman, that customers respond better to carrots than sticks, to respect than condescension. Fuller

believed he had The Answer to the world's problems – faith in God – but had learned that lasting commitment occurred mainly when people came upon answers in their own way, in their own time, with their own cultural inflections. He wanted, as a result, to build not Jordan's "demonstration plot for the Kingdom of God" but thousands of them, each built by people who might have been, in a previous generation, bitter enemies. Instead of saying "Have faith!" he would put down fertile soil in which faith might bloom.

To realize this vision, Fuller wrote, Habitat's supporters would have to become "monumental beggars." The phrase was used by Jordan eight years earlier, at the birth of the Fund for Humanity, and harks back to his conviction that the world's troubles were rooted in economic disparity – those with too much pursuing even more, those with too little suffering until they rebelled. Fuller had come to agree: at some level he saw his former, millionaire self as the "snarling wolf trying to get his little bit of carcass" – Jordan's description of American economic life. But Fuller had lived and thrived in the money-changing world, and knew that thousands of business people, properly approached, could be Habitat allies. (See photos on following page for a sampling of corporate Habitat supporters.) *Clarence knew I felt empty despite success, because of all that money...and I can't be the only rich guy with a hole in his soul! If Clarence could make the New Testament accessible to illiterate sharecroppers, can't we make Habitat's mission accessible, acceptable, to John Q. Businessman and his friends?*

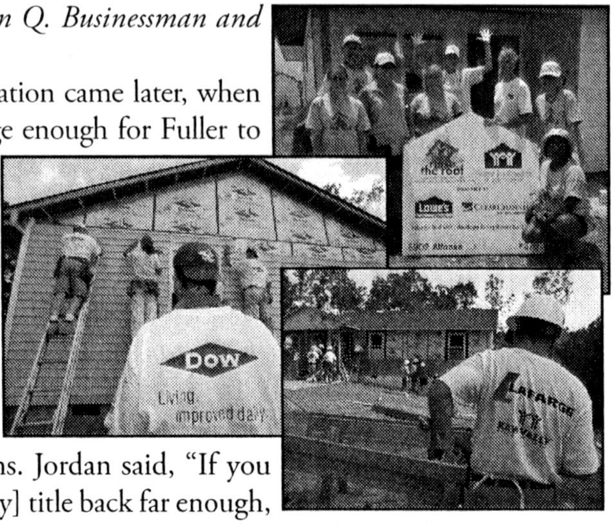

But that realization came later, when Habitat grew large enough for Fuller to catch his breath, to think more strategically. In the beginning, he stuck much more closely to his mentor's message, if stating it in friendlier terms. Jordan said, "If you trace the [property] title back far enough, somebody stole it"; Fuller wrote, "the poverty of the '*have-nots*' is directly related to the riches of the 'haves'" (emphasis in original), that there's "a direct line connecting the two- and three-house person with the no-house person." Fuller has been criticized for watering down Jordan's message, but it's fairer to say he took out the truculence, or tailored the message for different audiences, which Jordan – not one to sugar-coat, despite Koinonia's dependence on pecan candy and fruitcake sales – never did.

For all that, though, Fuller still quotes Jesus' admonition that "It is easier for a camel to go through the eye of a needle than for a rich man to enter the kingdom of God." (At right, what would happen if lawyers worked the Pearly Gates.) Fuller's presentation has evolved, however, becoming more polished, more feel-good, more media-friendly as Habitat became a star in the non-profit firmament. Having struck a cultural nerve as well as a social need, Fuller began talking in the mid-1980's of the "theology of the hammer," a philosophy centered on the 'economics of Jesus' and which turned Habitat away from the implicit socialism of Koinonia. But the idea remains a vibrant, optimistic restatement of Jordan's faith-in-action thinking, a vision in which words are solely

"Fine – we'll get a bigger needle."

prelude. Christians might disagree on baptism and communion and clerical clothing, Fuller wrote in 1986, but all could agree on the gospel's exhortation that Christians serve their fellow man.

"Not too many years earlier," Fuller wrote in 1980 about Habitat's founding, "I had set myself a goal: to become a millionaire as quickly as possible. Now my life had new goals. Could we be so bold as to think of building enough houses for a million people?" That goal, laughable when set to paper, was met in 2005...and most of Habitat's projections to date, it should be noted, have proved conservative.

Eight

"For the Mutual Benefit of All Persons"

I should stand around more. I hate standing around, particularly on Habitat sites, because it makes you feel useless, ineffectual. *If I wanted to do nothing, I would've stayed home, eh?*

But standing around does give you the chance to observe and absorb, to think. And what I've been thinking, recently, is that Americans associate "being busy" with "being important." How can you be trivial when you're juggling three phone calls, two clients, and a now-or-never deal? People want to talk to you, need to talk to you, want to do business as soon as possible with you – and therefore your work *matters*. Doesn't it?

We're on Hanover Street in Bridgeport again, but this time we're working on a duplex. It's near the intersection with Seeley, and the place is a complete wreck – until recently, a crack house. "We've already been through that place a couple of times," says Allen Marx, stopping by to gauge our progress. "You should've seen the needles we picked up."

I'm standing around waiting for things to appear – the tool-bearing Habitat truck, the metal-only dumpster, the crew from Fairfield's Sacred Heart University (some student regulars are shown on the previous page, working on a different house). I'd rather be working full-bore, but Jeff Carter, Bridgeport Habitat's Construction Manager (and no relation to Jimmy), has asked me to supervise the crew with Angel…and Angel, after dropping me off, has left for a parent-teacher meeting. I've been kicked upstairs, in short, but that's okay: I'm forced, against my natural inclination these days, to think.

The Hanover neighborhood, though sadly neglected today, must have been wonderful a century ago. The house I worked on with Tom and Frank, Fred and Allen and Mario, I'm now convinced is a genuine Palliser, designed by a forgotten architect who made a specialty of affordable housing. George Palliser, an English carpenter, emigrated to the U.S. in 1868, and by the following decade was designing block after block of "worker" housing for the City of Bridgeport. And they were beautiful houses, too – inventive, detailed, colorful, sometimes charismatic. Palliser set a high standard for the town: other builders followed, so wrap-around porches, constantly changing rooflines (lots of dormer windows, as shown on page 114), and arresting details (fish-scale shingles, vivid shutters) are a fairly common sight in Bridgeport today, even on modest homes.

How did Palliser's influence have such reach? He had a powerful patron: P.T. Barnum – yes, *the* Barnum, the showman remembered for saying "There's a sucker born every minute." That attribution is now doubted…and I believe the doubters, because history has given Barnum a raw deal. He's legendary for his salesmanship, his museums

and circuses and shows and "humbugs," but his biggest creation was Bridgeport itself. The town existed before Barnum moved here – in part to be close to Tom Thumb (shown at left, with Barnum), whom he "discovered" in Bridgeport – but became significant only after he built "a new city" across the Pequonnock River, noting the area's deep-water port and strategic location (midway between Boston and

New York). Yes, he sold sizzle rather than steak…but Barnum, far more importantly, practically invented modern affordable housing. He realized – half a century before Henry Ford revolutionized manufacturing by following the same insight – that the working class could be customers as well as employees.

In the 1840's, already rich from promoting sideshows (below, a dozen Barnum elephants test a new iron bridge), curio museums, European tours, and himself through a best-selling autobiography, Barnum decided to settle in Bridgeport, once called the "prettiest village" in the state. But he wasn't a fellow to stand around: he thought Bridgeport ideal for industrial development, and in 1851, with partner William Noble, bought 224 acres he would christen "East Bridgeport." He laid out streets, planted trees, put in a large public park, then announced his intentions – to sell every other lot on the condition that a "suitable dwelling-house, store, or manufactory" be built on the property within a year. And he primed the real-estate pump by selling the lots at slightly above cost – without profit, in essence – to anyone with sufficient dollars. Well, almost anyone, whether individuals, companies, retail stores, or manufacturers: Barnum insisted on sensible architectural designs, house setbacks, fences, and "other conditions which would render the locality a desirable one for respectable residents, and operate for the mutual benefit of all persons who should become settlers."

Barnum called the project "profitable philanthropy," and making money on it "a secondary consideration." Barnum's words should always be taken with a bucket of salt…but the comments ring true, in part because the self-described "Prince of Humbugs" was out-humbugged by a crafty clock manufacturer for whom he signed financial notes. Barnum had to declare bankruptcy, but subsequently redoubled his efforts to turn Bridgeport into the state's finest city, and by the 1860's lot prices had increased from $200 to as much as $4,000 an acre. Barnum and Noble took their profits; by 1864, when old Bridgeport absorbed Barnum's "new city," the combined area boasted nearly a hundred manufacturing companies employing more than 3,000 workers. Forty years later Bridgeport was the industrial center of the U.S., validating the motto it adopted when Barnum served as mayor in 1875 – "Industria Crescimus," or "by industry we grow."

Did Barnum's housing plans draw Palliser to Bridgeport? It's impossible to say: perhaps Palliser saw Barnum's 1864 advertisement in the *Bridgeport Standard* headlined "Every Man to Own the House He Lives In." The notice offered loans at six percent interest to fifty "industrious, temperate and respectable individuals, who desire to build their own homes" in East Bridgeport. No "reasonable plan," the ad said, would be turned down…but Barnum had his own blueprints, and would put up a standard house (after selling the lot at a "fair" price) without further profit. "[N]ice dwellings, painted, and furnished with green blinds," Barnum continued,

> can be erected at a cost of $1,500 or $1,800, for house, lot, fences, etc., all complete, and if six or eight friends prefer to join in erecting a neat block of houses with verandas in front, the average cost need not exceed about $1,300 per house and lot.

An accompanying newspaper article noted that unskilled workers rarely receive such offers, adding that while Barnum might profit from the deal, "it will be by making others richer, not poorer; by helping those who need assistance, not by hindering them…."

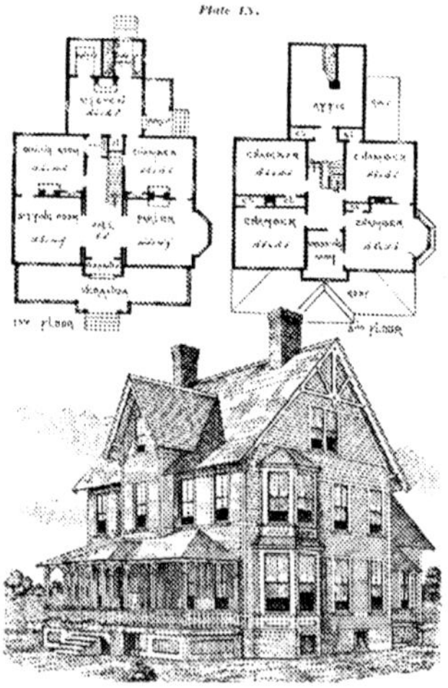

Barnum built not only row houses, increasingly common in the East, but single-family homes as well. And he frequently offered cheap, long-term financing for both land and construction, because the arrangement "enabled many persons to secure and ultimately pay for homes which they could not otherwise have obtained." Why, he asked, should the working stiff pay a landlord when rent money, put toward mortgage payments, in a few years made him an owner? The American Dream of home-ownership predates the

American Revolution, but Barnum was among the first to make it accessible to the average American family. Between 1846 and 1886, according to the long-defunct *Standard*, Barnum's name was on 1,637 real-estate transfers, the majority for homes.

If Barnum advanced Palliser's home-building career – made him, in effect, Bridgeport's "house architect" – Palliser ensured his place in history by encouraging people to build their own homes. (On the previous page, "Residence of W. Coe, Stratford, Conn." from the self-published *Palliser's Model Homes.*) He put his designs to paper, and – borrowing a page from Barnum – marketed them through a score of "pattern books" that made "Every Man a Complete Builder" (so reads one subtitle). The ambitious handyman would buy a pattern book, select a design – anything from a three-story, turreted, $3,000 home to a simple, two-room, $325 cottage – then purchase the plans and specifications directly from Palliser & Co., Architects, Bridgeport. After George brought in his brother, Charles, the company was renamed Palliser & Palliser and moved to New York City.

Palliser's American Cottage Homes (1878) consists, the author wrote, of "practical designs of low and medium priced houses suited to the masses of our country." To modern eyes, though, the plans are wonderfully expressive, with form obviously related to function, if not following it. One nine-room, $2,600 house, for example, is said to be "finished in a very plain manner"...yet has a back porch, a two-sided front veranda, a dining room lit by a hexagonal bay window, a library, four fireplaces, and complicated, steep-angled roofs. As George Palliser notes in another pattern book – a sentence quoted on a number of architecture-firm websites – "[I]t is not expense and ornate decorations, which so many ignorantly believe to be the highest attainment of architecture, but design, which produces true beauty and graceful appearance."

And Palliser's influence on home-building doesn't stop there. Besides demystifying and democratizing the architectural profession, as one historian has observed, the brothers legitimized "mail-order architecture"; established the first correspondence course in architecture; and inspired Sears, Roebuck and Montgomery Ward to develop "homes by mail" catalogues, essentially dolled-up pattern books. Sears' Modern Homes Department (on the next page, the cover of its first catalogue)

sold some 100,000 such homes between 1908 and 1950 – including Jimmy Carter's boyhood home in Archery, Georgia (built by the original owner, not a Carter). The provenance of many Sears homes, often cited for their high quality, was discovered only in the late 1970's, when the pool of run-down Victorians grew scarce and bargain-hunters had to look harder for rehab properties. George Palliser, given his debt to Barnum, would laugh to learn his ideas proved far more durable than his name.

Palliser eventually decamped to New York's Westchester County, there to fall off the historical map. Though most of Bridgeport's Pallisers have been torn down, and most of those remaining are in disrepair, his designs can still be found throughout North America, from Seattle to Chicago, Ontario to Newfoundland. So perhaps it's true: books can inspire people to move from armchair to action, from complacency to creation, to see words as the first step, not the last.

The Hanover duplex may have been built by Barnum himself. He once owned the property, according to a century-old map posted in the Bridgeport library: Seeley Street takes its name from one of Barnum's grandsons, and we're a block from Iranistan Avenue, named after Barnum's first Bridgeport mansion (he built four). Iranistan itself, pictured in a postcard at left, would burn to the ground in 1857...but not before Barnum put in numerous access roads and avenues, so locals could enjoy the landscaped grounds and, not coincidentally, view his biggest self-advertisement.

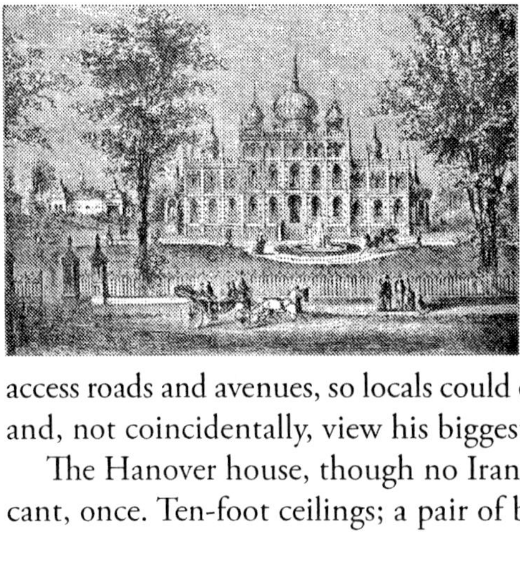

The Hanover house, though no Iranistan, was something significant, once. Ten-foot ceilings; a pair of bay-window alcoves in front, their margins decorated with plaster scrolls; a huge plaster rosette in each parlor from which chandeliers hung. But this history is history: we're going to gut the house, and this craft-work won't survive.

The place is a burn-out. There's a hole in the floor six feet across: the wood's charred edges smell acridly of burned paint, the basement holds yards and yards of wet pink insulation. Who knows what caused the blaze – an overtaxed electrical system, a fire started for heat, insurance-fraud arson, the making of crack or crystal-meth. On any given day in Bridgeport you can drive past a dozen forgotten burn-outs, so this neighborhood's lucky: the re-building process has begun.

I tour the house. It's not in terrible shape: most of the walls can stay, though they'll have to be re-wired and re-plumbed. The house will need new staircases, too: the existing ones won't meet code, and aren't wide enough for today's furniture, anyway. What really cries out for repair, though, is the roof, for the old rafters have pulled away from the peak by as much as three inches, and there's no ridge beam, either. The bathrooms? The toilets overflow with human excrement, residents having used them for weeks after the utilities were turned off. This was not, I realize, just a crack house: people lived here 24 hours a day. For some it was a kind of home…but now they've gone, effectively evicted by redevelopment, the working poor displacing the even more marginal.

Cars pull up and park, and so does the truck. Some Sacred Heart students, Habitat regulars, know the drill, and the sidewalk is soon covered with shovels, hammers, wheelbarrows, rakes, crowbars, hard hats, sledgehammers.

Demolition is the perfect job for students, a great way to learn about home construction while burning off young-adult energy. (Demo is called "our Favorite Chore" on the Sacred Heart Habitat website: below, Sacred Heart students in a Habitat Dumpster.) But it's not a free-for-all, what with sledgehammers swinging left and right, two-by-fours tossed from windows. And it's potentially costly, too. "Make

sure you show them how to pack a dumpster," Jeff had said back at the warehouse: every dumpster-haul adds hundreds of dollars to the cost of a house. Which is why that metal-only dumpster is on site: the plumbing, the water heaters, the radiators can be recycled. Bridgeport Habitat even recycles stone, a local cement company picking up ledge and rocks and asphalt, free, to grind into concrete for an I-95 rehab project. Habitat homeowners have driven across stone that once sat beneath their house.

My job, as I've self-defined it, is to remind the hard-working students to take breaks and rehydrate themselves – it's a warm day – and to find tasks for those with a tendency to goof off. We're pushing water heaters out a basement window when Angel returns to say our priority is removing the old lathe and plaster, the heaviest construction debris; shovel it into wheelbarrows, and we can roll the plaster right into the dumpster's open end. Soon half the students are happily smashing walls.

Angel (shown at right) motions for me to follow him into the eastern parlor. "I learned this last time," he says. "Watch."

He picks up a flat-bottomed shovel and slams it into the wall with a low DiMaggio swing. Small cracks spider-web from the impact on the smoke-blackened wall. Angel takes a couple steps, swings again, and a second web intersects the first. Plaster rattles down inside the wall; Angel's fourth swing takes out an irregular, baseball-sized divot, and the wall begins to bow out. At the sixth blow the wall vibrates, and on the seventh it explodes like a virus-infected cell, sending dust and chunks of plaster, in a hundred sizes, everywhere.

"You do it like that, you don't have to work so hard," says Angel. "But be careful," he adds, glancing at the ceiling: "Make sure everyone wears a hard hat. Jeff's orders."

Easier said than done, both the work and the rule-enforcement. Angel, for one thing, has hard-pack muscles from his other job, landscaping: he builds many rock walls, admires the shape and look and weight of stones, often carries a few in the bed of his truck. And although he's only five-five, Angel looks like a major leaguer, all bulging forearms, when choking up on the shovel and hitting the wall a dozen times in quick succession – *whap whap whap whap whap whap* – in the wake of a couple lay-off-the-slider check swings. His stroke is sharp, compact, controlled, because a focused swing, I saw, breaks the lathe/plaster bond. My own whacks had made deep dents in the plaster, from which I could lever off loosened sections with the shovel blade; Angel brought down half a wall with less effort, for he let gravity do the work.

We took a few walls down that morning. Before lunch I tried my hand at the parlor ceiling, and hoped to spare the central rosette, but swinging a shovel over your head is not a precise art. The blade, propelled by my uncertain, cactus-league swing, bounced off the ceiling, hit the rosette, and chipped a plaster flower basket.

An Antarctica-shaped chunk of plaster, four feet by six feet, landed on my head a minute later. Revenge, perhaps? The sound, as it struck my hard hat, was impressive; students appeared in doorways, tracking the reverberating *fooshhhh.* I tried to laugh off the incident, but coughed as plaster dust rose toward the ceiling, as if to reapply itself.

By noon everyone was exhausted. The students broke for lunch, as they'd brought drinks and sandwiches in a cooler; I keep working, having forgotten to coordinate a diner ride with the regulars down the street. If we push, I decide, we could fill the dumpster by the end of the day...and immediately feel the tension in every Habitat affiliate (every organization, really) between workers and management. *If these strong backs would spend less time flirting, take fewer so-called water breaks, we could meet the schedule, we could get these families in by August....*

The afternoon brings more of the same, and by quitting time, the dumpster's full. Angel gives me a ride back to the Remington complex, and asks if I mind stopping by his house to drop off some storm-door hardware. I don't: in fact I want to see where he lives, never having worked in Bridgeport's East End.

It's a rough neighborhood, by U.S. standards. Angel lives down the street from a notorious social club, the Yellow Bird, where muscle-bound bodyguards give strangers the once-over: you wouldn't want to drive by the club at night, let alone walk. The area is so bad, in fact, that a nearby Habitat home has stood empty for months. "We showed it to one lady," Angel says, "and when she leaves this guy's pissing outside the door. Who wants to live where this guy's getting a blow-job right there? I've seen it, they don't even try to hide what they're doing."

His mood changes as we approach his home. "My house, I love it," he says, pointing out the short stone wall he's building alongside the driveway. I'm about to say many of my suburban neighbors are putting up stone walls, too – I'm glad to find Angel and I have more than Habitat in common – but stop myself. Angel is staking a claim by building his wall, he has something truly dangerous to keep out; my neighbors are creating ersatz history, and invariably hiring coffee-skinned day-laborers to do the grunt work. I later learn, on a Habitat build in Asuncion, Paraguay, where *sudamericano* masonry skills come from, for we put in rock foundations. With a little thought, a lot of patience, and an aptitude for finding the proper stones – we took to describing the desired stones as looking like Idaho, or Utah, or Switzerland – you could fill any gap, any hole, any need.

When we turn onto Newfield Avenue, I glance at the front of the house and finally make the connection. I've seen it in photos: nothing particularly distinctive, just a baby-blue Victorian with a small, neat yard protected by a cyclone fence. But the house is special, for the actor Paul Newman helped build it in 1996.

Bridgeport Habitat reveres the actor, who lives in neighboring Westport, because his one-day presence put the affiliate on the map. Hundreds of locals followed in his footsteps: politicians, business executives, community leaders were suddenly anxious to jump on the Habitat bandwagon. Newman (that's him in the photo at right, carpenter's pencil in his mouth, working on the Newfield home) seemed to understand the idea behind Habitat better than some regulars, telling reporters

the organization represented "the opposite of rugged individualism." It was a sly comment on his own image – particularly since he was swinging a hammer with a hand wrapped in gauze bandage, the legacy of a recent car accident.

Angel deeply appreciates Newman's contributions to Bridgeport Habitat, financial as well as morale-boosting, but he's ready to stop hearing about "the Newman house." Angel turns and says, "It's my house," and I understand, for the first time, how complex Habitat homeowning can be.

Nine

"Interested, or *Very* Interested?"

Habitat for Humanity was officially incorporated in November 1976, four months after the Fullers' return from Zaire. It would be headquartered temporarily at Koinonia, with the understanding that the new organization would soon move to Americus, less than three miles away. Habitat and Koinonia were close kin, clearly, but their visions had diverged, and those involved felt the groups' identities should be kept separate. The farm was about red clay and equality and living in harmony: the new non-profit was about change, synergy, finding common ground.

Fuller, as noted, thought the Habitat formula well-suited for rural areas and Third World countries where land, in particular, was cheap. Affiliates could be started with very little money – the "barriers to entry were low," as Fuller might have said in his business days – while the chance of success was relatively high, since affiliates faced little competition in very-low-end home construction. But when a friend from Koinonia asked Fuller, then still in Zaire, whether a Fund for Humanity project might work in the slums of San Antonio, Texas, he didn't hesitate. "The determining factor," he replied, "is not geography or population density; it is trust in God and faithful adherence to the economics of Jesus."

The San Antonio Fund for Humanity, in Texas, was incorporated before Habitat for Humanity itself, and would become Habitat's second chartered affiliate (after the 'home team' in Americus). The trail it blazed (logo, at right) would be followed by most affiliates, including those in Danbury and Bridgeport, and would bring heartache and frustration as well as many home dedications. Consider the typical growing pains: little construction knowledge; poor build sites; lack of money; personality clashes; government red tape; broken promises; vandalism and thievery; community skepticism and, sometimes, outright opposition. But San Antonio, like most affiliates, displayed the essential dedication – from Christian radicals and Sufi-influenced Quakers, Princeton-educated missionaries and Central American immigrants – to put in the thousands of hours of sweat and blood that home-building, and affiliate-building, required.

The founders of the San Antonio affiliate argued and backtracked, regretted their rashness, grimaced at terrible ideas and the occasional unhelpful volunteer. But they stuck with it, because Fuller assured them that the houses would eventually get built. Habitat, after all, was on a mission from God. "People are learning that with a little faith they can move mountains," Fuller wrote the affiliate's prime mover, Birdie Lytle, as the not-yet-affiliate worked to complete its first home. "Just keep on asking for what you need. Keep precipitating those crises and asking people to help you solve them.... Run out of money and call for help!"

Lytle and her colleagues got creative, as Fuller suggested. *Many people give ten percent of their income to support their church's good works, they noted. Maybe some would tithe to support homeowner-built housing, or donate ten percent of something else to ensure their neighbors had decent shelter?* Lytle's band of builders ran the idea up the Habitat flagpole, and people responded. A local real-estate agent donated ten percent of his commissions; a few families pledged to match ten percent of their house payments. A certain passage from Matthew became popular around the San Antonio Habitat office, the one that goes – in the Cotton Patch Version – "Start asking and it will be given to you; start looking and you will find; start knocking, and the door will be opened to you."

The money came in, slowly, and land was found, slowly. San Antonians continued to show up and volunteer – intrigued at first, then surprised, pleased, and many, ultimately, infected with Habititis. The man with an earth mover who cleared that first build site; the contractor who ran a work crew, cut deals on building materials; the neighbors who formed a family-selection committee. The future home-owners weren't hard to find, either, for San Antonio's west side was a slum, occupied largely by Hispanic immigrants. The Torres family – mom, dad, four kids – would live in that first house, their $85 monthly mortgage paying for taxes, insurance, utilities, and the home itself. Ernesto Torres, a house painter, sometimes fell behind on his payments – bad weather meant no work – so the affiliate restructured the mortgage...and Ernesto helped paint the affiliate's second home.

A group in the Appalachian hills of Tennessee formed the next affiliate, soon followed by groups in Johns Island, South Carolina (the affiliate has produced a book celebrating its 25th anniversary, cover shown at right), and Immokalee, Florida. Their stories begin with the same question: *Hey Millard, you think a Habitat project might work here?* And it usually did, despite the customary complications, because enough people had enough energy, and faith, and commitment, to see a house through to completion.

Kansas City, Missouri; Paducah, Kentucky; Denver, Colorado; Tucson, Arizona. Through word of mouth, and the press, people throughout the U.S. heard about Habitat, and asked if they, too, could try the experiment. Habitat spread like a grassfire, a virus; like the pebble tossed in a still lake, making no great splash itself but causing waves on every shore. As it happened, though, the ripple only needed to reach a peanut warehouse in Plains, Georgia, ten miles to the south.

Jimmy Carter knew a thing or two about being poor. As a child Fuller helped rehab a sharecropper's shack, but the future president had slept in one; he'd experienced windows without glass, porous

floors and walls, broadsheet "wallpaper" applied with flour-and-water glue. Five such shacks sat a stone's throw from the Carter family home, and young Jimmy stayed in Jack and Rachel Clark's shack (a replica at the Jimmy Carter Boyhood Farm is shown at left) whenever his parents were away. Carter doesn't call the Clarks a second set of parents in his memoir *An Hour Before Daylight*, but he might as well have: the boy followed Jack Clark around as he tended the horses and livestock, and often played checkers, or went fishing with, Rachel Clark. Jimmy, at the Clarks, slept on a mattress stuffed with corn shucks or wheat straw, which he'd drag, on cold nights, in front of the fireplace.

Carter, growing up, knew about Koinonia Farm, but didn't give it much thought until leaving the Navy in 1953. After his father's death he returned to Plains and started a farm-supply business...but soon discovered, like Koinonia, that the freedom he'd defended through public service wouldn't be afforded him at home. (For a time, he also lived in public housing in Plains – photo of Apartment 9A at right.) Asked to join the racist White Citizens' Council – and remembering his childhood was "shaped by black women," that Rachel

Clark, far more than his parents, "talked to me about the religious and moral values that shaped a person's life" – Carter refused. His warehouse was boycotted; as late as 1965 the John Birch Society spread rumors that Carter, by then a state senator, was a Communist. (When Carter, as head of the Sumter County school board a few years earlier, tried to integrate the local high schools, he was greeted at the peanut warehouse one morning by a sign reading, "Coons and Carters Go Together.") Carter didn't help Koinonia during the 1950's, its darkest days, but in the 1960's he sold the farm seed, processed its peanuts, and opened the Plains schools to its children when Americus refused to accept them.

Fuller tried to recruit Carter for Habitat after the 1976 election. It seemed a no-brainer, for Fuller at least, since the two men shared populist, south-Georgia, born-again-Christian roots. But Carter had Washington to deal with, an entire nation, and didn't respond...at which point Fuller publicly lambasted the president for being "not adequately concerned about the plight of poor people" (as Carter characterized the criticism). It was a rare mis-step by Fuller, an "ugly episode" in Carter's view, but one he got past when friends, visiting the White House, raved about their experiences building with Habitat in Zaire. An excellent carpenter himself, Carter knew how empowering the building process could be, especially when you used your own hands.

Carter heard more after returning to Plains permanently in 1981, when Habitat regulars flocked to his Bible class at Maranatha Baptist Church (which had split from another church over its resistance to integration). Fuller knew he'd been forgiven when Carter accepted an invitation to address the Habitat board. Carter subsequently sent a substantial check...and Fuller realized he might be able, after all, to land this very large fish.

In early 1984 Carter agreed to a one-on-one meeting. Fuller drove to the Carter home in Plains, was received by both Jimmy and Rosalynn, and quickly went into sales mode: he thanked the Carters for their previous support, their attendance at various Habitat events. At last he came to the closing pitch: "Are you simply *interested* in Habitat for Humanity," Fuller asked, "or are you *very interested*?"

Carter grinned, at the very least intrigued, and possibly shocked, by Fuller's audacity. But Carter knew his Bible, about Koinonia and Clarence Jordan and the Fund for Humanity, and even, perhaps, Jordan's remarks about 'spiritual pygmies' and the need to 'think big.' Carter looked at Rosalynn and replied, "We're *very* interested."

Two weeks later Fuller sent a note outlining 15 ways in which the Carters could help Habitat, such as writing letters and volunteering on site, introducing Habitat to influential people and praying for the organization's success. On his return visit Fuller expected to find Carter had selected three or four items, but Carter said, in essence, he'd do them all. Telling the story today, Fuller invariably adds, "I wish I'd put a hundred things in that letter!" Carter served on Habitat's board for many years, and Fuller notes that the former president "never missed a meeting, never came late, and never left early."

The seriousness of Carter's commitment became apparent the following year, when he traveled to Manhattan to give a sermon. In the course of a morning jog he stopped by a six-story Habitat rehab project on East Sixth Street (at right, the dedication ceremonies) and thought, "Rosalynn and I should come up and give them a hand." Only then did Carter realize he wasn't thinking to himself but talking out loud – and had been overheard. Minutes later he was inside the building saying, yes indeed, he'd be willing to help. The local Habitat director replied, "Why don't you come back with a group from your church for a work-week?" and the Jimmy Carter Work Project was born.

"That first year we didn't know if we could get any volunteers to pay their own way," Carter later wrote, referring to the $150-per-person expenses. But many Plains and Americus church-goers did sign on, recognizing a once-in-a-lifetime experience (so it seemed at the time). The concept was improbable, almost laughable – *a former president working in a ratty tenement, for an entire week? Hammering away, sweating alongside housewives and clerks and cashiers? Staying in a bunk bed in a church, eating institutional food, sharing a common bathroom?* But outlandishness was, of course, the idea's great strength. The event would be a living parable, irresistible even to a jaded media.

The bus left Habitat headquarters on September 1, 1984, with Carter, the Fullers, and 16 other volunteers on board. Another 18 people boarded in an Atlanta suburb: many of the new passengers were journalists, including a *New York Times* reporter whose account of the ride would run on the front page. The following morning, after stopping for an impromptu Sunday service at a very surprised New Jersey church, the crew arrived in Manhattan. They drove to the abandoned six-story apartment building...and the professional builders in the crew immediately said – in chorus, Carter later wrote in his book *Everything to Gain* – "It can't be done." The skilled volunteers (others, at right, shown marching into Manhattan from Brooklyn) were

"discouraged almost to the point of resentment that anyone – they all looked at me – could have thought of bringing them so far to be part of an absolute fiasco."

Carter's solution, back at the church, was to ask the most experienced carpenters to have dinner at his table, and then how they'd approach the rehab if they decided to continue. "Soon," Carter wrote,

> they were competing with each other to outline the best plan for how our group could be divided into teams, which tasks had to be performed first, what additional materials we would need, and how much might be accomplished while we were in New York.

Carter showed that any problem – with enough people, time, and good will – could be solved. The first step was the hardest: moving from fear to faith, from words to deeds.

On Monday the tenement held as many reporters as volunteers (a few even stayed to help out). Walls came down, flooring came up, rotten beams were replaced, a new roof put on; by the end of the week the

demo pile had grown to the top of the second floor. The volunteers were led, at times, by professional carpenters – a direct result of Carter's involvement, for a union leader had threatened to picket the site because Habitat, he said, was taking jobs away from working tradespeople. Fuller called Carter (shown above at the Sixth Street site), who called the official and said the union should be *helping* to build affordable housing, not hindering it. The union backtracked, subsequently donated money and drywall to the project, and at the end of the week, gave Carter a gold union card.

That first 'Jimmy Carter Work Project,' as it came to be known, would change Habitat forever. The Times story was just the first of a flood, and you couldn't watch national television that week without seeing, at some point, an interview with Carter or Fuller. The media's typical theme was that Carter, and Habitat, were doing something not merely eccentric but extraordinary. *Former U.S. Presidents don't work up a sweat – they take it easy, they cash in! They travel in style, not on buses; they talk with dignitaries, not the poor; they try to rehabilitate their own reputations, not someone else's falling-down home! Something's wrong here...unless, of course, it isn't....*

Journalists, skeptical toward Carter's emphasis on morality and faith, started to come around. They couldn't help themselves; Carter was often the first volunteer on site, worked late, and used chalk lines and speed squares, chop saws and spirit levels, with authority. Carter was leading by example, not posing for photo ops: was challenging couch potatoes to get up and help less-fortunate neighbors. When a reporter asked Carter, "What made you sacrifice a week to come here instead of going to the Virgin Islands?" the response was direct and plain-spoken. "It's not a sacrifice," he said. "I'm enjoying it. It's great to meet new friends and do something to help others at the same time."

The phones at Habitat affiliates everywhere, especially in New York and Americus, rang off the hook. Millions of people who had never heard of the organization were now saying to themselves, *Hey, if it's good enough for a former president, it's good enough for me.* The effect of Carter's involvement is evident at Habitat headquarters – a red-brick, refurbished auto dealership on Americus' main drag – where an enormous timeline charts the organization's growth. There's a notable upswing in the mid-1980's...which is why, when veteran Habitat volunteers refer to the "B.C." time period, they usually mean "Before Carter."

Neither Carter nor Fuller expected the work project to be repeated. But as with any home construction, the early enthusiasm waned. When Carter, by then a Habitat director, heard the East Sixth Street rehab had fallen seriously behind schedule, he offered to make a return engagement (on top of chairing a campaign that would raise $12 million, far more than Habitat had ever raised before). The second work project, in 1985, drew nearly as much publicity as the first, in part due to novel marketing techniques. The local Habitat affiliate suggested local churches "hire" Carter by the hour, and one man, hearing the former president had put in 51 hours, donated more than he expected. He wrote a check for $1500, calculating that Carter had also put in eleven hours at time-and-a-half pay.

Carter now works with Habitat, formally at least, one week a year. Since the mid-1990's he's been part of crews building in Illinois; North Carolina; Pennsylvania; Wisconsin; California; Florida; Maryland; Ontario, Canada; South Dakota; Hungary; Kentucky and Tennessee; Texas; the Philippines (where homeowner Leonisa Salas said she would never forget that the former U.S. President's sweat was holding her home together, since it was, quite literally, in the mortar); New York, Georgia, and Florida; South Korea; South Africa; Alabama and Georgia; and Mexico. Within a few decades the Jimmy Carter Work Project will have built houses – thousands of them – in every state in the union and in close to a hundred nations around the globe. And as long as he is physically able, Carter will be there...an idea I can attest to, since I've seen Carter at work in Harlem, New York, and in Durban, South Africa. He likes getting his hands dirty, and would much rather walk than talk.

Ten

Block and Circus

It's your basic high-rise beach resort – we could be in Florida. The hotel is a comfortable, 1970's Holiday Inn, and you half expect to see flared jeans and Janis Joplin t-shirts. The bus is like any other, its passengers could be from anywhere, and we look through the windows at grocery stores, boutiques, touristy restaurants. I don't feel unsettled, out of context, until we reach the jobsite, perhaps five miles from central Durban (the city's beach area, above, seen from the hills), a vacation-and-port city on the east coast of South Africa. We eat breakfast under huge white canvas tents, listen to a couple of speakers, walk down the road to the staging area...and realize we're part of a military operation. We're going to build an entire village, 100 houses, in five days.

We're out of our minds. This is a job for professionals, clearly...but we amateurs, nearly 5,000 of us, will get it done, come hell or high water. Edmund Hillary climbed Everest "Because it's there"; we Habitat volunteers are building this neighborhood "Because it isn't there, and should be."

I've lived in London and Taipei and Santa Barbara, seen elephants in India and lions in Kenya; I've skied Tahoe, the Rockies, British Columbia; I've piloted airplanes, scuba-dived, built a car from a kit; I've hiked in Madagascar, gotten lost in the Sierra, witnessed riots in Paraguay. But this is a real challenge; it's not about me and my limits but the exact opposite, almost – it's about forgetting myself, me and my self-centered goals. I'm a soldier fighting for the right side, free of doubts, and that alone gets my endorphins going.

I can turn off my brain and work, follow orders, knowing that woman over there – or maybe it's this one, I've yet to meet Amelia Maisenyane or her son, Mthokozisi – will soon have something to celebrate. A house with a door, not a bedsheet; a floor, not a mud slick; a tile roof, not something fashioned from a 55-gallon oil drum. We saw some of Durban's shantytowns driving in from the airport – hovels of tin and cardboard and recycled wood scraps, some as large as beach cabanas (Patience Lisa's former home, above) – and being but a stone's throw from the city's up-to-the-minute abundance, they are a shocking reproach. Nearly half of South Africa's population, more than 20 million people, lives in substandard housing, which means more than 1 million in the Durban area alone.

Cato Manor, on the banks of the Umkhumbane River and named after Durban's first mayor, was first settled in the early 1900's by East Indians, who'd been brought to Africa by the English to work in the sugar-cane fields. The Indians eventually rented and sold shacks to native Africans, for in Cato Manor, unlike more urban areas, some non-whites were permitted to own land. The blacks and Indians, 40,000 strong, lived in relative harmony until the 1940's, but racial tensions developed, in part because Indians had much greater economic success. Activists – following in the steps of longtime Durban resident Mohandas Gandhi, politicized in 1893 after being thrown off a train for occupying a first-class compartment – quoted a common joke: the Europeans arrived carrying the Bible while the natives held the land, but soon the natives carried the Bible and the colonists held the land.

Race relations worsened with the creation of apartheid in 1948. When the government, in the 1950's, decided to move natives to segregated areas, police were called in. The residents of Cato Manor resisted, white policemen were killed; the settlement was razed, and blacks were sent to segregated housing developments. Cato Manor (above right, the portion terraced for Habitat homes) remained undeveloped ever since, despite its proximity to Durban, its hillside location and expansive views. But the property's fallowness was deliberate: each South African race – "colored" Asians, black Africans, white Europeans – was to have unimpeded, independent access to the city, so Durban's suburbs were developed in wedges separated by highways, railroads, utility lines, open space. Habitat, in the Sherwood section of Cato Manor, was building in no-man's land yet again...and as in Zaire, would re-christen it with a new spirit. Sherwood (the nearly completed Habitat project, above left) is now known as "Ethembeni," Zulu for "a place of hope."

The theme of the 2002 Jimmy Carter Work Project, for obvious reasons, was "reconciliation." South Africans of both Indian and Zulu descent would be living in peace once more, this time in solid houses with electricity, running water, and flush toilets, all built by volunteers hailing from 50 countries. "Here," said Durban Mayor Obed Mlaba at the opening press conference, "we are stitching together the scarred landscape left by apartheid."

I've come with Jerry, my hotel roommate, who's a regular volunteer back in Ohio. He works for Goodrich, which I take as a good sign, and slightly resembles David Letterman, though his sense of humor is even drier. I can't tell, at first, when Jerry's joking and when he's serious...but then again, I'm not much good for anything right now, between the jet lag and the 5 a.m. wake-up call. We're supposed to be at our assigned house by 7, and work until the day's tasks are done...even if that means tearing down a poorly built wall and putting it back up again.

I looked through the sheaf of volunteer handouts on the bus, and as usual with Habitat International publications, they're first-rate. Lots of photos, maps, charts, illustrations, explanations: a marketing-package-cum-volunteer-celebration, showing how quickly land of little value can be transformed into something priceless. But I'm most anxious to get my hands on the construction manual, the 26-page, photo-copied-and-stapled building bible. Leave the four-color, beautifully designed press kits for fly-in, fly-out journalists: I'm sleeping with the construction manual under my pillow, because I want to build this house right.

Habitat advance crews have already put in roads; poured concrete foundations; installed water, sewage, and electrical systems, including, for night work, huge sodium lights on twenty-foot poles. We'll never have to stay up until dawn, hopefully – but this is a blitz build, *boom boom boom*, the process screeches to a halt if we miss daily deadlines. The electricians can't work until the walls are up; the plumbers can't do *their* job until the bathrooms and kitchens are just about complete. The upside? Most of the tradesmen will be working at night, with few volunteers to get in the way.

The build schedule is, in a word, back-breaking. *Monday*: Put up all the exterior concrete-block walls, including the windows and door frames. *Tuesday*: Erect the trusses (instructions below), install the roof purlins, tile the roof, put up the battens, paint the exterior. *Wednesday*: Build the wood-frame interior walls, insulate the "attic" (with blueboard donated by Dow), drywall, tape, and compound the walls and ceilings, cut and install the gable cladding. *Thursday*: Finish drywalling, sand and re-compound the drywall, install trim, and first-coat paint the interior. *Friday*: Install doors, finish painting, complete touch-ups, landscape, work around the licensed plumbers, and clean up site for the late-afternoon dedications. And every day we try to practice our pidgin Zulu – "Hello" is "Sawubona," "Thank you" is "Ngiyabonga," "Did I do it right?" is "Kuhle?" – to generate a few international laughs.

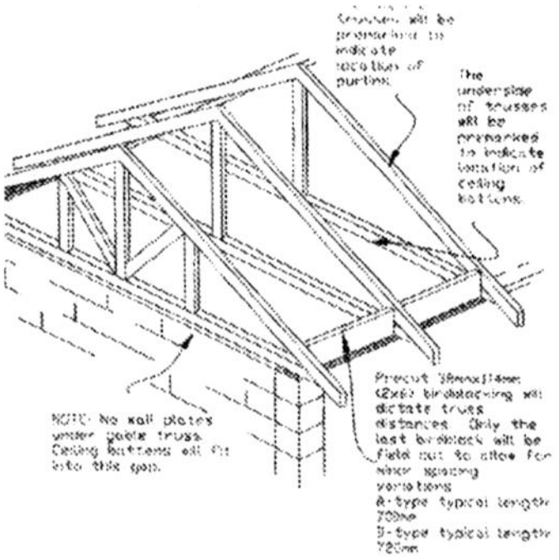

Figure 1: Truss Layout (not to scale)

It takes a village, apparently, to build a village.

We start by laying block. I used a technique learned in Guatemala: while working on a home in the Mayan village of Tacajalve, my roommate Jorge and I (George was his real name, and he looked more like a rock-and-roll roadie than a banker from Brooklyn) got better results laying mescla with the back side of a trowel. (Right, the family we worked with in San Francisco, of which Tacajalve is a suburb.)

Dip, dig, swing, *splat*: it's extremely satisfying when you find the rhythm, when the mortar hits the block just so, when you've scooped up just the right amount of mortar, at just the right consistency. We'd tried buttering the blocks first, as initially instructed, but we didn't have the arm strength to sling blocks one-handed, for hours, as the locals did. If our technique seemed to work, the crew chief wasn't going to complain.

In Durban the mortar was mixed in large pits shared by half a dozen houses. The consistency was more regular, the mixture more precise: in Guatemala the crew chiefs often stinted on cement, because it was expensive, and sometimes on sand, perhaps because we had to sift it ourselves from a load of pebbly beach sand previously delivered by truck. Durban was beginning to feel like a "luxury" build: mescla available as needed, all kinds of tools lined up in a shipping container next to the house, "service" volunteers coming by regularly to dispense water, snacks, lunch. Professional builders never had it so good!

For some reason I'd never gotten a house assignment, so I ask my hotel roommate, Jerry, if I could work on "his" house, Number 905. He was a crew leader – issued the telltale yellow ballcap – and naturally agreed. Jerry had led a number of Global Village trips, and knew that much Habitat "building" is in your head, because you're creating a team, an attitude, as well as a home. On one Central American trip a hurricane stranded his crew for days in a single large room without electricity and little food. "I woke up one night to the sound of crying," Jerry said. "Some people really lost hope." No houses were built on that trip – but a few middle-class

Americans, back home, had a better appreciation of how much of the world lives.

We have a good "core" crew, from all over the States – California, Idaho, New York, Georgia, Virginia – and various African countries. I team up with Geofrey Isingoma (yes, only one 'f' in his given name), a Habitat staffer from Uganda, but we soon discover the crew

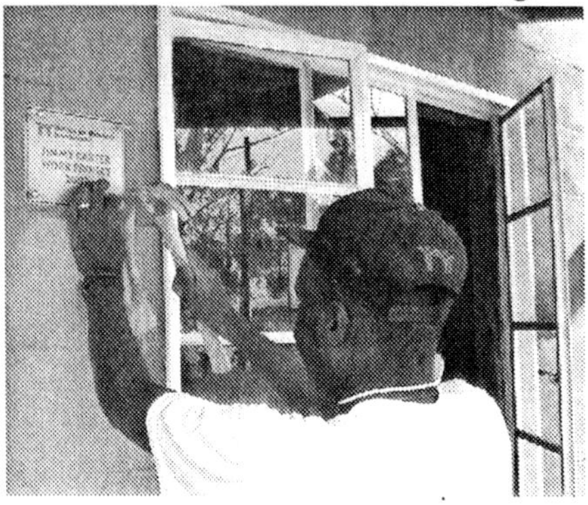

– sometimes numbering eight (too few), sometimes 30 (far too many) – has better block layers; they set four blocks for every one of ours. (That's Geofrey, left, putting up the sign when Number 905 was almost complete.) The skilled block-layers are generally Zulu, and many are professionals, though whether they're building as volunteers or as homeowners, I never resolve. Our own homeowner – Amelia's a security guard, a common job in South Africa because of carjackings – will make mortgage payments of perhaps $30 a month, or about 25 percent of her income. It's a good deal...even if her new home has less square footage than my living room back home.

From the crew on the next wall I hear familiar conversations.

"How's it look over there?" says Jen, from California, moments after placing a block. She taps the block – much narrower than those used in the Caribbean or Central America, which must withstand earthquakes and hurricanes – with a trowel handle, looking for perfection.

"Not too bad," Lyn replies, putting a four-foot level horizontally along the wall, spanning three blocks. It doesn't rock, so the wall is straight, though it might be bowing out or in, or tilting some. "Maybe another tap?"

A homeowner named We stops by the site – other names we encounter are Patience, Urban, and Knowledge – and begins to sing a Zulu song. She's wearing a blue construction jumpsuit, though never does a lick of work, so far as I can tell; but no one cares, because she's got this huge, infectious grin, and it's a pleasure to hear her sing. Lucille, a 20-year-old South African of Indian descent, joins in: she's the crew's self-appointed morale officer, her effervescence keeping spirits up even when the work seemed endless, or goes wrong. We didn't have to rebuild an entire wall, as one team did, late into the night...but we could've, with Lucille and her English accent urging us on.

Jen taps the block. Lyn nods, gives a thumbs-up.

There's an unspoken competition with the other teams, on your own crew and on the other houses. (Part of the crew, at right, from left: Jen, Lala, Lala's niece Lucille, Jerry, Lyn.) You want to build faster, better, neater...and the rivalry, strangely, seems to bring everyone together. Because the main "winner" is the future homeowner? Perhaps. I don't detect personal agendas, just the desire to work hard, have fun, contribute. Jeez, we're acting like adult Scouts!

Jen and Lyn high-five each other. I peek at the level: the bubble's dead center, couldn't be deader.

With most of our wall done, and Geofrey taking a break, I wander the site. I thought my Global Village experience would give me a feel for things, but the JCWP is totally different; it's huge, fast, organized. (Below, a model Habitat house standing behind the kind of house it replaces.)

Working in some village with a small Habitat group, you're the circus come to town, the week's entertainment: here we're worker ants, building practically non-stop, and the locals entertain us. They break into song at the drop of a hat, clapping and dancing, and you find yourself moving, swaying, without conscious effort. Groups of singers, 40 strong and mostly women, march down the street in full voice, making musical instruments superfluous. We have no idea what they're singing, but the joy – completed by the colorful dresses, bright as the sun – is infectious. We'd sing along, if we knew how.

Mambo Mkhize's house is about as far from 905 as you can get. I wander down the hill, but not to meet her, in truth: like many volunteers, I'm dropping by Number 1000 to catch a glimpse of Jimmy Carter. I'd shaken his hand at the end of the 2000 JCWP, where I'd worked for a day at the 134th-Street building in Harlem (a Secret Service agent volunteered to take a picture of the crew, and Carter, with my camera). The former president always tours the project site, tries to meet every new homeowner and volunteer...but only after the houses are done. Work comes first: you can see Carter's impatience when he's sitting for interviews, when he's compelled to speak. As he had said at opening ceremonies, "There's a time for photographs, and

there's a time for work." (Above, work crews from a number of houses, including 905, have their picture taken, post-build, with Millard and Linda Fuller, Jimmy and Rosalynn Carter, the new homeowners, and fellow volunteers.)

Carter is easy to spot, since so many other people are looking for him. He's laying block on the far wall with his son Chip, and they're cruising along; not as fast as the Zulus, no, but way faster than Geofrey and I. Maybe I'll build Habitat walls with my own son someday – when Matthew's in his twenties, unsure of what to do with his life, or after we've grown apart during his college years. Chip hands his father the level, who puts it on the row of blocks, and they lean back on the scaffolding to admire, and possibly correct, their work. I think of a Zulu idea I learned a day earlier – "ilima," often translated as "working together for a common purpose."

Many eyes well up at dedications, often when the homeowner bursts into tears while accepting the key to her new front door. I've also teared up at such moments...but I'm surprised to find my vision going blurry now, while looking at the Carters, at Mambo's house. I'm missing my own family, sure, but I'm also seeing what it means to live by example, to live your faith.

...and suddenly I'm back in Paraguay. It's September 11, 2001, our second morning in Asuncion, and we're lugging rocks for foundations when a young man walks up and says, 'Nuevo York?' Living less than 90 minutes from Manhattan, I say 'Si!' ...but that's the limit of my Spanish, so I direct him to Craig, a Los Angeles-based architect with fluent Spanish. The men talk, then disappear into the shack we were replacing. (Right, Griselda, whose Habitat house we also worked on in Asuncion.)

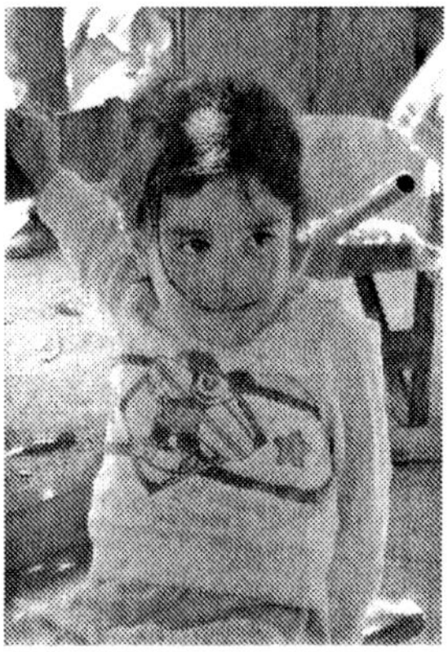

Soon the homeowner emerged, carrying a television, which he set on a plastic chair against the outside wall. *Guess they want to keep us entertained*, I think, until I see the grim faces on every local. The screen flickers on, talking heads speak in Spanish...and then we see the videotape from lower Manhattan. Asuncion shares New York's time zone, so the news is fresh: the World Trade Center had been attacked by terrorists, the twin towers were crumbling to the ground. We didn't need Spanish to realize we were witnessing mass murder, that our world would never be the same.

No one will forget the horror, the disbelief, of that day. But what I remember, above all, is that we dozen *norteamericanos* were soon back at work. Not because we were untouched, unaffected – many of us had relatives in New York City and Washington, D.C. – nor because we needed to keep busy. No: we were back at work by 11 o'clock – mixing mescla, moving stones, cutting up stumps, digging trenches, stacking blocks – because our work proved the terrorists wrong.

This was the America I belonged to: citizens paying thousands of dollars of their own money to become day-laborers in a far-off country, to help people they didn't know, would never see again. For the next week we were front-line anti-terrorists, building lives – according to Paraguayan plans, to meet Paraguayan needs – rather than destroying them. The result, I believe, is a stronger Paraguay, a stronger America, and stronger people wherever Habitat puts down roots. I can't say that working with Habitat caused me to have faith in God…but it has, without question, given me faith in the human race.

Postscript

On January 31, 2005, Millard and Linda Fuller were fired by the Board of Directors of Habitat for Humanity International. A few weeks after Millard's 70th birthday, the Fullers were kicked out of the organization they had spent 30 years – nearly half their lives – building into one of the most respected non-profit organizations in the world.

Habitat volunteers were shocked to the core. It seemed improbable – *Millard was* fired? *How could the board* do *that?* The explanation seemed unlikely, too: Habitat's founder had been accused of "inappropriate personal behavior," as the board put it – of sexually harassing a married Habitat employee during a long car ride to the Atlanta airport in 2003. Veterans of international Habitat builds were quick to excuse Fuller, knowing that global experience can result in touchy-feely behavior: when you don't speak the local language, you end up putting arms around shoulders, slapping thighs, giving hugs. *Surely Millard, who had traveled to scores of countries on Habitat's behalf, who understood the power and symbolism of physical contact, had been misinterpreted? Trying to step beyond American chauvinism and aloofness, to bring some Latin-African-Caribbean warmth back home, he'd forgotten the American need for personal space....*

At first I, too, believed Fuller's angry denials, despite knowing that similar charges had been lodged against him more than a decade earlier.

In the early 1990's Fuller's job was saved in large measure by Jimmy Carter, who warned that Habitat could be seriously damaged by a sexual-harassment scandal, and hinted he might quit the organization himself if Millard were terminated. Responding to the current scandal, Fuller claimed the Habitat board was trying to push him out because he pictured the organization continuing to grow and reach out, while the board wanted Habitat to retrench and solidify its base. Fuller, indeed, had been at odds with the board, on and off, for years: like many entrepreneurs and visionaries, he was better at initiating than managing, at inspiring than strategizing...and didn't like people looking over his shoulder. When I asked Fuller, years ago, if I could follow him around for a week while researching this book, he brushed off the idea, saying he spent most of his time dictating letters.

Habitat staffers and long-time volunteers girded themselves for the media onslaught. The "he said, she said" stories; the "where there's smoke, there's fire" opinion pieces; the outraged defenses of Fuller by upset supporters, and the sad-but-we'll-move-on justifications by current Habitat executives. The flood, however, never arrived: only a trickle of stories appeared, mostly torn from the newswire, as if this was one battle, one scandal, America didn't need. Perhaps journalists remembered the media circus surrounding Jimmy Swaggart and Jim Bakker in the late 1980's, when the supposedly old-fashioned televangelists were caught in sexual improprieties with women not their wives...and decided that Fuller, whose ministry had helped millions of people in obvious, lasting ways, deserved a different fate.

But *The Washington Post* pursued the story, and in March published a front-page article that destroyed any chance of reconciliation. Reporter Alan Cooperman found a number of sex-related skeletons in Fuller's closet, and the pattern they created was extensive, difficult to dispute, and stretched back to Fuller's time at Koinonia Farm. Two former Koinonia leaders told Cooperman that Fuller had had extramarital affairs while at the farm, and that counselors were brought in to help him deal with his 'issues': one of those leaders, Christopher Bugbee, also noted that a female Koinonia volunteer had complained about unwanted sexual advances from Fuller. "The discovery that his private conduct was at such odds with his public preaching," Bugbee told Cooperman, "destroyed the trust between Millard and the rest of the Koinonia leadership" and led directly to Fuller's departure. The incident mirrors Fuller's split with Habitat – as does Fuller's telling the Post he made "mistakes" at Koinonia but denying that indiscretions forced him to leave.

Cooperman also located one of the five women who accused Fuller of sexual misconduct in 1990 (some of whom received significant compensation packages when they resigned). One of the women, a Habitat International volunteer before her hiring as Habitat's director of training in 1986, was quoted as saying, "What people know who worked with Millard for a long time was that this behavior was very prevalent." A Habitat staff chaplain in the late 1980's came close to confirming that statement when she told Cooperman "easily four or five other [Habitat employees]" complained about Fuller's behavior during exit interviews, but didn't want to confront him in person. Both women quoted in the Post article are identified by name.

Fuller, on seeing the article, protested. Using his considerable legal skills, he wrote a letter to the editor, subsequently published by the *Post*, saying that Cooperman

> allowed my detractors to dredge up 35-year-old hearsay and unproven allegations, apparently without making an effort to talk to the large number of women I have worked with throughout my career who would have taken issue with these character attacks....

It was "false," Fuller continued, to say he was terminated due to sexual harassment, because Jimmy Carter – who spend many months trying, once again, to broker a settlement – had resulted in a document saying "there was 'insufficient proof' of inappropriate conduct on my part." Moreover, Fuller wrote, "logic would dictate that if I had been fired for sexual harassment, there would not have been cause to fire my wife, Linda." Perhaps...but it's as easy to imagine Fuller confessing to Clarence Jordan that he was a "female-holic" as well as a "money-holic."

Fuller has subsequently founded a new organization, the Fuller Center for Housing, with which he intends to continue his decent-shelter work. In June 2005 – after first calling the charges against him "baloney...[the Habitat board] treated it like I had possibly killed the woman" – he told the student newspaper of his *alma mater*, Auburn University, that

> a billion people in the world live in sub-standard housing, and Habitat for Humanity is currently building something over 20,000 houses a year, and they have a plan to go to 30,000 a year in the near future....But even at 30,000 houses a year, which is way more than they're building now, it would take 7,500 years, at the current level of need, to build all the houses that are needed. So it seems obvious to me that help is needed, and that's what we in the organization want to offer – help."

Fuller's vision and drive, clearly, remain intact.

And so, of course, does Habitat for Humanity. At this writing – June 22, 2005 – volunteers are siding 30 houses in and around Detroit, Michigan, as this year's Jimmy Carter Work Project winds down. And I'm printing out budget forms and recruiting new volunteers for my next Global Village trip, to the northern, more touristed coast of the Dominican Republic. . .four weeks after returning from my last GV trip to the DR, Housatonic Habitat's annual 'Tropical Build' in Paraiso. As always, our Habitat crew – travelling from one of the richest parts of the Western hemisphere to one of the poorest – discovered that building tiny houses with the locals can be a lot more fun than consuming, collecting, keeping up with Joneses, and shopping at the mall; that sharing with others can be far more rewarding than focusing on your industrialized self, your individual wants, your cultural 'needs'.

We timed that trip to coincide with Dominican Independence Day, when many towns have Mardi-Gras-like *carnavals.* Our crew, after four trips now a part of Paraiso life, was pressed to participate: Jesulin, one of our many local "keepers," brought an aqua sheath dress for me to wear, and also a local artist to paint our faces with Dominican and U.S. flags. As we marched along the village's narrow, noisy streets, I noticed that hundreds of spectators – blowing whistles or cracking bamboo-frond whips, singing songs or just laughing at the silly costumes and the *loco Americanos* – fell in step with the group as we passed by. And it struck me, once again, that Habitat isn't so much about building houses as breaking down barriers; of making sure everyone, absolutely everyone, has enough.

For two decades I've longed to vacation at one of the Dominican Republic's sun-and-fun resorts – to windsurf at Cabarete, swim at Puerto Plata, scuba dive at Sosua. But those trips will have to wait, because there's too much to be done: too many houses to build, too many people to help, too many opportunities to express faith in fellow human beings. Right now, in the velvet grip of Habititis, I feel the need to infect others, as that's as close as I'll come to living childhood fantasies of being a superhero. No, volunteering with Habitat isn't "saving the world"...but it's something, and I can sleep at night.

Acknowledgements

Like Habitat itself, this book is the product of many partnerships. Above all I'd like to thank the scores of Habitat homeowners, volunteers, and supporters I've worked with over the years (and sweated with, too), for this is their story. I'd also like to thank the Habitat personnel who have helped me, especially those who sat down for interviews (Millard Fuller) or agreed to look at the manuscript (Housatonic Habitat Executive Director Chris Brown, Bridgeport Habitat's CEO Bob Knebel, Habitat's NorthEast Coordinator Bruce Rogers). My one-time editor Hugh van Dusen suggested the title (though I still like "Talk is Cheap"); my one-time agent Jim Hornfischer came close to selling the project to a major publisher, but perhaps we were ahead of the curve.

I'd also like to thank my parents for giving me the confidence – or perhaps the recklessness – to take on another oddball project: for that I feel very lucky. My brothers, likewise, did yeoman service: John, a painter and website designer, put the cover together, and David, a Chinese-language typesetter and printing consultant (Birdtrack Press), walked me through the production process with incredible patience. We Goodrich brothers make a pretty good team!

Lisa Miles, my wife, read countless revisions of the manuscript as I tried to capture an experience that doesn't translate well to the page. Her support and editorial comments were invaluable, even when I didn't take them. And the kids – Thea, Matthew, and Hayley – were always there to make me laugh when writing about Habitat seemed both endless and pointless (and also type labels, stuff envelopes. add stickers...). It's true, I love playing with Habitat kids on Global Village trips, but I always come back to my own family!

Many people also read the manuscript in galley form and helped eliminate countless silly mistakes – readers who include my parents, my sister Anne Heck, Chris Mulia, Pablito Almira, Vin Masotta, and others, I fear, who have slipped my mind at the moment. My apologies to all, and I beg forgiveness.

As a former legal reporter, I've attempted to establish facts with certainty, but in a few places I've interpolated, New-Journalism-style, where it seemed appropriate. Errors that have resulted from this approach, or from occasional sloppiness or overconfidence, are my sole responsibility.

Illustration Credits

Overture

Page viii – Working on house 'deck' in Danbury. Credit: Chris Mulia

Introduction

Page xii – Monticello: stone house (slave quarters), September 1770, by Thomas Jefferson. N38; K16 [electronic edition], Massachusetts Historical Society, Coolidge Collection of Thomas Jefferson Manuscripts.

Page xiv – Jimmy and Rosalynn Carter at the New York City Jimmy Carter Work Project, 2000. Credit: Chris Goodrich

Chapter One

Page 2 – Millard Fuller in Las Vegas, 2004. Credit: Eric Jamison / Habitat for Humanity International

Page 3 – Girl with bucket in Tierra Blanca, Guatemala, 2001. Credit: Denise Muschel / HfHI

Page 4 – Patch Street house before demolition. Credit: Chris Goodrich

Page 4 – Pablito sanding. Credit: Chris Mulia

Page 6 – Monticello's West Front with larkspur. Credit: Thomas Jefferson Foundation.

Page 8 – Luxury home pictured at www.swineotopia.com

Page 8 – John Locke portrait. Credit: FoundingFathers.info

Page 9 – "A Map of the Most Inhabited Parts of Virginia...." 1755 reproduction of 1752 original by Joshua Fry and Peter Jefferson. Credit: Library of Congress

Chapter Two

Page 14 – Linda Fuller at Koinonia in 1971. Credit: HfHI

Page 16 – Clarence Jordan at Koinonia. Credit: HfHI

Page 17 – Ku Klux Klan rallying in Atlanta, Georgia, in 1937. Source: "Brief History of the Ku Klux Klan, Focusing on Their Use of the Flag, by Jeffrey Todd McCormack, at www.pointsouth.com/csanet/kkk.htm

Page 18 – "Freedom Riders" on bus headed South. Source: The Freedom Writers / Freedom Ride 2005, www.gruwellproject.org

Page 20 – Clarence Jordan and Millard Fuller at Koinonia. Credit: Habitat for Humanity file photo

Page 22 – cover of "Black Like Me," hardback edition 2004. Source: Wings Press, San Antonio, Texas, www.wingspress.com

Page 23 – detail from postcard of Norton Hall, Southern Baptist Theological Seminary, Louisville, mailed in 1918. Source: Old Louisville Guide, www.oldlouisville.com

Page 25 – Florence and Clarence Jordan at Koinonia, 1946. Credit: pjb/cjg / Lenny Jordan / HfHI

Page 26 – Stained glass rosette window with "Koinonia superimposed. Source: Amherst Koinonia Church in Massachusetts, www.amherst-church.com.

Page 28 – Koinonia peanut field. Source: Carol and Larry Tebo, www.tebotales.com

Page 28 – Mule-drawn wagon at Koinonia, probably 1940's. Credit: pjb/cjg / Lenny Jordan / HfHI.

Page 29 – "Ku Klux Klan Kismet" songbook. Source: "Brief History of the Ku Klux Klan, Focusing on Their Use of the Flag, by Jeffrey Todd McCormack, at www.pointsouth.com/ csanet/kkk.htm.

Chapter Three

Page 31– First edition of *Flatland*. Source: www.eldritchpress.org.

Page 32 – Sphere-passing-through-plane illustration from *Flatland*. Source: www.eldritchpress.org

Page 32 – Sphere perspective from *Flatland*. Source: eldritchpress.org

Page 33 – A Philo Curtis Road house seen through the window of another. Credit: Chris Goodrich

Page 35 – Larry Coleman working in Newtown. Credit: Chris Goodrich

Page 37 – Housatonic Habitat's first house, on Danbury's Elm Street. Credit: Chris Goodrich

Page 39 – Sign protesting low-income housing in Bethel, Conn. Credit: Chris Goodrich

Page 41 – Roger Authers headshot. Credit: Chris Goodrich

Chapter Four

Page 45 – Millard Fuller analyzing Koinonia Soil. Credit: Koinonia Partners Inc. / HfHI

Page 46 – Koinonians on a truck, 1940's or 1950's.

Page 43 – Senator Joe McCarthy. Credit: U.S. Senate Historical Office

Page 48 – Emmett Till. Credit Mamie Till Mobley / The Chicago Defender

Page 49 – Dorothy Day in 1968 (flipped image). Credit: Milwaukee Journal / Marquette University Archives. Source: www.rain.org/campinternet/american-history/peace-studies/women-peace-history-1.

Page 50 – Clarence Jordan on courthouse steps. Credit: HfHI

Page 51 – Millard Fuller, 1969. Credit: Linda Fuller / HfHI

Page 52 – Clarence Jordan at his typewriter, 1961. Credit: pjb/cjg / Lenny Jordan / HfHI

Page 58 – St. Augustine, pictured in The Hundred Greatest Men, published by D. Appleton & Company, 1885. Source: Medieval History Site, www.historymedren.about.com

Page 59 – Modern cover of *Clarence Jordan's Cotton Patch Gospel: Luke and Acts*, Smyth & Helwys, Macon, Georgia. Credit: Smyth & Helwys, www.helwys.com

Page 61 – Koinonia house-building sign and "Fund for Humanity" houses, 1979. Credit: HfHI

Chapter Five

Page 64 – Remington shot tower at Bridgeport Habitat warehouse. Credit: Chris Goodrich

Page 67 – Four typical Bridgeport burn-outs. Credit: Habitat for Humanity of Greater Bridgeport, www.bridgeporthabitat.org

Page 68 – Roof work on a Bridgeport rehab. Credit: Habitat for Humanity of Greater Bridgeport, www.bridgeporthabitat.org

Page 68 – A Bridgeport Habitat home during rehabilitation. Credit: Sacred Heart University, Campus Chapter, Habitat for Humanity

Page 68 – Operating the 'manlift' at a Bridgeport Habitat home. Credit: Sacred Heart University, Campus Chapter, Habitat for Humanity

Page 70 – Allen Marx. Credit: Habitat for Humanity of Greater Bridgeport, www.bridgeporthabitat.org

Page 70 – Cutting Hardiboard® (measure ten times, cut once). Credit: Sacred Heart University, Campus Chapter, Habitat for Humanity

Page 71 – Using the guillotine. Credit: Sacred Heart University, Campus Chapter, Habitat for Humanity

Intermission

Page 78 – A modern "Cotton Patch Gospel" poster. Credit: Dramatic Publishing, www.dramaticpublishing.com

Page 79 – Tom Key in a 2004 "Revelation Project" in South Carolina. Credit: Michelle Attaway, North Greenville College "Skyliner," www.ngcskyliner.com/news/2004/04/21/News/Tom-Key.Performs.During.the.Revelation.Project-665831.shtml

Page 83 – A drawing of the demon Mammon in Collin de Plancy's 1826 "Dictionnaire Infernal." Credit: www.grand-grimoire.com/demonologie/monarchie_infernale.htm

Chapter Six

Page 90 – A girl doing homework in her Habitat home in San Cristobal, Guatemala, in 2001. Credit: Denise Muschel / HfHI

Page 91 – Lorenzo, a Habitat volunteer and the "mayor" of a Paraiso barrio, with children. Credit: Rebecca Tate

Page 92 – A roof pour in Paraiso, 2004. Credit: Vin Masotta

Page 93 – Mixing a mescla volcano, 2004. Credit: Chris Goodrich

Page 94 – Moving roof cement with wheelbarrow. Credit: Vin Masotta

Page 95 – Vin Masotta shoveling from the deck. Credit: Ted Clark

Page 95 – The after-dinner entertainment at the Hotel Paraiso. Credit: Chris Mulia

Page 96 – Wendy and Pilar, 2004. Credit: Chris Goodrich

Page 96 – Three girls on their porch. Credit: Jean DaSilva

Chapter Seven

Page 99 – Setting block in Mbandaka, Zaire, in 1976. Credit: HfHI

Page 100 – Henry Morton Stanley in pith helmet. Credit: London Stereoscopic Company / www.de.wikipedia.org

Page 101 – Map of Zaire. Credit: CIA Factbook, www.cia.gov/cia/publications/factbook

Page 102 – Mobutu on throne. Source: www.un.int/drcongo/history

Page 102 – King Leopold II of Belgium. Source: www.worldroots.com/brigitte/royal/royal16a.htm

Page 103 – Mbandaka Habitat houses, 1981. Credit: wv / HfHI

Page 104 – Linda and Millard Fuller in Zaire, 1974. Credit: HfHI

Page 105 – Tom Sawyer whitewashing fence, drawing from Tom Sawyer, 1876. Credit: The Mark Twain House, Hartford, Conn, found at www.pbs.org/marktwain/learnmore/writings_tom.html

Page 105 – Drawing of Prospero contemporary with Beerbohm Tree's Production of "The Tempest," 1904. Source: www.leeds.ac.uk/english/staff/projects/treestempest/images

Page 106 – Original cover of Bokotola, produced by New Win Publishing in 1978. Source: Bookpeople, www.bookpeople.com

Page 107 – Fuller at Habitat ceremony in Zaire, 1982. Credit: HfHI

Page 108 photo grouping – Dow team working in Anniston, Alabama, 2003. Credit: Gregg Pachkowski / HfHI

-- Lafarge volunteer working in Anniston, Alabama, 2003, Credit: Gregg Pachkowski / HfHI

-- Clear Channel employees with homeowner, San Antonio, 2004. Credit: Steffan Hacker/ HfHI

Page 108: Original cartoon involving camel, lawyer, needle, and Pearly Gates. Credit: Tony Dangerfield

Chapter Eight

Page 111 – College students on scaffolding. Credit: Sacred Heart University, Campus Chapter, Habitat for Humanity

Page 112 – P.T. Barnum with Tom Thumb. Source: National Portrait Galley, Smithsonian Institution, www.npg.si.edu

Page 113 – Page from Joel Benton's 1891 Life of Hon. Phineas T. Barnum showing elephants testing a bridge in Bridgeport. Credit: Charles Keller, Lisa Spiro, University of Virginia Library Electronic Text Center, www.etext.lib.virginia.edu

Page 114 – Page from *Palliser's Model Homes, Showing a Variety of Designs for Model Homes* (1878), showing a Stratford, Conn., house. Credit: reprint, Glenwood Publishers, Felton, Calif.

Page 116 – Cover of the first Sears Modern Home catalogue, 1908. Source: www.oldhouseweb.com/stories/

Page 116 – Page from Joel Benton's 1891 *Life of Hon. Phineas T. Barnum* showing Barnum's Iranistan mansion. Credit: Charles Keller, Lisa Spiro, University of Virginia Library Electronic Text Center, www.etext.lib.virginia.edu

Page 117 – Sacred Heart student loading Dumpster. Credit: Sacred Heart University, Campus Chapter, Habitat for Humanity

Page 118 – Angel Hernandez. Credit: Habitat for Humanity of Greater Bridgeport, www.bridgeporthabitat.org

Page 120 – Paul Newman working on a Habitat house in Kentucky in 1991. Credit: Julie Lopez / HfHI

Chapter Nine

Page 124 – Logo of San Antonio Habitat for Humanity. Source: www.habitatsa.org

Page 125 – Cover of Sea Island Habitat book. Source: www.seaisland-habitat.org

Page 126 – Replica of the shack lived in by Jack and Rachel Clark at the Jimmy Carter Boyhood Farm. Source: Jimmy Carter National Historic Site Education program, www.sowega.net/~plainsed/vtour/farmtour

Page 126 – Jimmy and Rosalynn Carter's public-housing home in Plains, Georgia. Source: www.sowega.net/~plainsed/kidsite/timeline.htm

Page 128 – The apartment-building site of the first Jimmy Carter Work Project, New York City, 1985. Credit: pjb/cjg / HfHI

Page 129 – Marching from Brooklyn to work at the first JCWP. Credit: wv / HfHI

Page 129 – Jimmy Carter cutting a beam in New York City in 1985. Source: www.pbs.org/wgbh/amex/carter/gallery

Chapter Ten

Page 133 – Durban beach area from the hills. Credit: Alysia Peyton / HfHI

Page 134 – Former home of Patience Lisa and her family. Credit: Kim MacDonald / HfHI

Page 135 – Aerial view of Habitat site at Cato Manor, before building. Credit: HfHI

Page 135 – Aerial view of Habitat site at Cato Manor, after. Credit: George Hipple / HfHI

Page 136 – Truss installation instructions from Jimmy Carter Work Project 2002 manual. Credit: Chris Goodrich

Page 137 – Kids eating in their new Habitat home in San Francisco, Guatemala. Credit: Chris Goodrich

Page 138 – Geofrey Isingoma putting up the official dedication nameplate at the Cato Manor home's completion. Credit: Chris Goodrich

Page 139 – Partial crew, House #905. Credit: Geofrey Isingoma

Page 139 – Habitat house behind the shack it replaces. Credit: Kim MacDonald / HfHI

Page 140 – Three house crews with Jimmy and Rosalynn Carter, Millard and Linda Fuller. Credit: HfHI

Page 141 – A young Habitat homeowner, Griselda, in Asuncion, Paraguay. Credit: Chris Goodrich

"Faith at Work" t-shirt., Dallas, 2004
Credit: Trevor Kobrin / HfHI.

Interested in volunteering with
Habitat for Humanity? Then contact
the organization at 1-800-HABITAT,
or go to www.habitat.org. At the
website can you look up your local
affiliate, donate funds online, and
subscribe to Habitat newsletters.

Housatonic Habitat can be reached at 203-744-1340,
www.danburyhabitat.org

Habitat for Humanity of Greater Bridgeport
can be reached at 203-333-2642,
www.bridgeporthabitat.org

Habitat for Humanity's Global Village program
can be reached at 800 422-4828,
www.habitat.org/gv/

Photo: Thea Goodrich

Chris Goodrich lives in Brookfield, Connecticut, with his wife Lisa Miles and their three children – Thea, Matthew, and Hayley.

Printed in the United States
32321LVS00005B/1-81

9 780976 822103